HILLARY'S
ANTARCTICA

To James, Hamish and Chris,
who may hopefully one day experience
and treasure the spirit of Antarctic
exploration.

NIGEL WATSON

HILLARY'S ANTARCTICA

ADVENTURE, EXPLORATION AND
ESTABLISHING SCOTT BASE

TEXT
NIGEL WATSON
|
PHOTOGRAPHY
JANE USSHER

ALLEN&UNWIN
SYDNEY·MELBOURNE·AUCKLAND·LONDON

CONTENTS

PREFACE   7
INTRODUCTION   9

13
— ONE —
THE GENESIS
OF THE CROSSING
OF ANTARCTICA

17
— TWO —
POLITICS,
PREPARATIONS
& PARTIES

33
— THREE —
THE ADVENTURE
BEGINS

65
— FOUR —
LIFE AT SCOTT
BASE

89
— FIVE —
THE TRACTOR
JOURNEY

125
— SIX —
DOGS ON THE
PLATEAU

147
— SEVEN —
NORTHERN PARTY

159
— EIGHT —
FUCHS: THE
CROSSING FINALE

165
— NINE —
BILL'S FLYING
ADVENTURES

169
— TEN —
TRACTOR JOURNEY
2.0

173
— ELEVEN —
CONSERVATION
EFFORTS

209
CONCLUSION

220   TIMELINE
222   BIOGRAPHIES
231   ACKNOWLEDGEMENTS
232   NOTES
236   BIBLIOGRAPHY
237   ABOUT THE AUTHORS

'I don't think the English ever forgave me for that one.'

SIR EDMUND HILLARY

PREFACE

'I don't think the English ever forgave me for that one.'[1] With those words an elderly New Zealand man, in a moment of contemplation and insight, reflected on his youthful endeavour at the bottom of the world.

Edmund Hillary became a global sensation when, with Tenzing Norgay, he became the first to successfully ascend Mount Everest. The New Zealander's success, three days after the failed summit bid by his British teammates Tom Bourdillon and Charles Evans, was acclaimed and celebrated. Hillary was knighted. The ascent of Everest was a British expedition, Hillary was part of the team, and he had been asked to attempt the summit by the leader.

Antarctica was different. Ed and New Zealand were a support act to the British Commonwealth continental crossing party. By heading on to the South Pole and reaching it before the crossing party, Hillary exceeded his brief. His actions created tensions, unleashed a media storm and denied the British an historic first overland to the South Pole since Captain Scott. Hillary even had the audacity to achieve the feat using three farm tractors.

Nevertheless, in doing so, Ed Hillary added another fascinating chapter to the exploration annals of Antarctica and he and his expedition team laid the foundations for New Zealand's continuous, and increasingly important, presence in Antarctica.

These handmade scarves were knitted by the
Canterbury Women's Institute and presented to each
expedition member for use during the International
Geophysical Year and Trans-Antarctic Expedition.
Ed's scarf is now on display at Canterbury Museum.

ED HILLARY'S SCARF

INTRODUCTION

New Zealand's
southernmost house sits on the
shores of Ross Island. It is a small
wooden-clad building, more like a bach
or a crib, dating from the 1950s,
complete with a portrait of a young
Queen Elizabeth II hanging on the wall.
The building looks south over
a frozen sea of ice which rarely
breaks out.

In one room, a small green cylinder featuring a cog wheel sits on a shelf on a black stand. This humble object is overlooked by almost all visitors to the building. The instrument is a sledge-meter. It harks back to a world and a time before the invention of global positioning satellites. A sledge-meter was used to record distance, and was attached to a bicycle wheel towed behind a sledge. Measuring in miles, the figures on this sledge-meter read 2043. This tiny instrument shows the distance recorded by British surveyor Ken Blaiklock as a member of the epic first overland crossing of the Antarctic continent.

That journey was the Commonwealth Trans Antarctic Expedition, and the crossing took 99 days in the Antarctic summer of 1957–58. It is the reason this small building, together with New Zealand's Scott Base which looms large behind it, is present in Antarctica.

SLEDGE-METER

Commonwealth Trans-Antarctic Expedition member Ken Blaiklock's sledge-meter, used on the crossing of Antarctica in 1957–58.

At the heart of that endeavour was New Zealand's most famous son, Sir Edmund Hillary. As leader of the Ross Sea Party, Ed's determination and his actions in Antarctica, in support of this first Antarctic overland crossing party, created history. When he made his famous 'dash to the Pole' on Ferguson tractors, beating the crossing party, it strained friendships, created resentment that in some cases lasted a lifetime, and overshadowed some of the remarkable achievements of other support party members and scientists. It was, however, a daring gamble that reflected Hillary's bold spirit. This was the first party to reach the Pole overland since Captain Robert Falcon Scott and his men in 1912.

That small building, which was home to Ed and a pioneering group of adventurers in the late 1950s, still stands sentinel over half a century later, an outpost of New Zealand. Not just a physical legacy of New Zealand's first expedition to Antarctica, it is a touchstone for exploration, science and discovery on the world's most isolated continent.

This is its story.

Hut A, the first building at New Zealand's Scott Base on Pram Point, Ross Island. Featuring in the background are Mount Discovery (left), Brown Peninsula (centre) and the Royal Society range (right).

Dr Vivian Fuchs, pictured here at Plateau Depot.

THE GENESIS OF

THE CROSSING

OF ANTARCTICA

ONE

FOLLOWING PAGE: View across McMurdo Sound to the Scott Coast and the peaks of the Antarctic mainland.

The Commonwealth Trans-Antarctic Expedition (TAE) was an ambitious expedition to cross the Antarctic continent from coast to coast via the Geographic South Pole.

It was to be led by the Englishman Dr Vivian Fuchs. Known as Bunny, Vivian Fuchs was a geologist who had studied at St John's College, Cambridge. He had been a member of an expedition to Greenland in 1929 with the noted polar explorer James Wordie, who himself had served with the famed Antarctic explorer Sir Ernest Shackleton. Following expeditions in Africa and service in World War II, Fuchs was rising through the ranks of the Falkland Islands Dependency Survey.

Fuchs' middle name was Ernest, which was apt, for it was Shackleton who had first attempted a crossing of the Antarctic continent over forty years earlier. Shackleton's Imperial Trans-Antarctic Expedition never reached the Antarctic continent as their ship, *Endurance*, was crushed in the pack ice in the Weddell Sea, forcing Shackleton and his men to spend the next 17 months in an epic battle to survive and reach civilisation. Frank Worsley, the New Zealander who captained *Endurance*, played a vital role in the party's survival, navigating the lifeboat *James Caird*, dwarfed by the rough and frigid Southern Ocean, on the journey from Elephant Island to South Georgia. Considered by many 'the greatest polar story ever told', the saga of *Endurance* became legend.

What lay unspoken for many years was the greatest polar story *never* told: the gripping account

of Shackleton's Ross Sea Party. They were on the other side of the continent, oblivious to the predicament that Shackleton was in, tasked with laying depots to support the crossing party. The Ross Sea Party, with inadequate equipment, undertook what was at that point the longest sledging journey ever (in terms of elapsed time) in order to lay those supply depots. Three of the men of this party died. Most tragically, it was all in vain as not a step was taken by Shackleton's crossing party towards those supply depots following the loss of *Endurance*.

A generation on, the basic premise for crossing the continent still held. Firstly, Fuchs' party would need to successfully navigate through the pack ice in the Weddell Sea and establish a base — to be called Shackleton Base — once it reached land. Secondly, a support party, on the other side of Antarctica in the Ross Sea area, was needed to establish its own base, to be known as Scott Base. Essential to the

success of the entire crossing expedition, this support party also had to establish a route up on to the Polar Plateau. Once up on the Plateau, they would need to create a depot with supplies of food and fuel. Fuchs' crossing party would depend upon the depot, and the knowledge that there was a proven route back down to sea level and safety, in order to complete its epic goal.

Who would be chosen to lead the support party in such an endeavour? In the early 1950s there was no more famous explorer on the planet than Sir Edmund Hillary, the conqueror of Everest. Charged with oversight of a New Zealand support party from the Ross Sea, his involvement had the benefit of ensuring support from New Zealand for a high-profile British Commonwealth endeavour. It would also attract media interest. In a nice piece of symmetry, Hillary's boyhood hero was Shackleton. It seemed that Vivian Ernest Fuchs and Sir Edmund Hillary might be the perfect match.

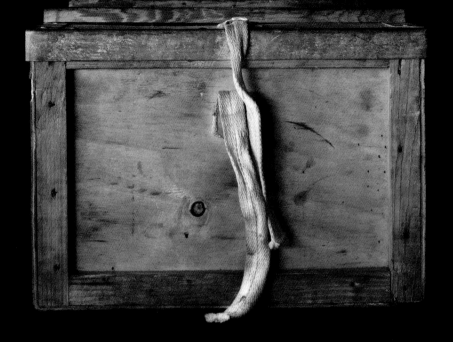

A wooden provisions box from the Trans-Antarctic Expedition, which is now part of the Canterbury Museum collection.

PROVISIONS BOX

POLITICS,
PREPARATIONS
& PARTIES

TWO

POLITICS

Fresh from his successful ascent of Mount Everest, Ed first met Vivian Fuchs in an unprepossessing little office in the middle of London towards the end of 1953. Ed was impressed with Fuchs' forceful personality and determination, the confidence of the man and the ambition of the project.[1] Although he was, at the time, committed to various projects in the Himalayas, and Fuchs had yet to raise funds for the expedition, Ed was interested in becoming involved should the project develop beyond an exciting idea. Hillary undertook to do what he could to create interest in New Zealand.

Two years later, in early 1955, Fuchs had succeeded in obtaining significant financial support from the British government for the Trans-Antarctic Expedition. There now remained the question of what support the New Zealand government would provide in terms of building a base in the Ross Sea. The timing coincided fortuitously with a growing awareness in New Zealand of the scientific and exploratory promise of Antarctica. In particular, there was increasing concern about the government's failure to exercise its sovereignty over the Ross Dependency, which had been claimed by New Zealand since 1923. There had been no official attempt to explore the Dependency and, apart from a bureaucrat with the rather grand title of 'Administrator of the Dependency', successive governments had simply ignored the issue. In contrast to New Zealand's inertia, the Americans were becoming more and more active in the area and had already, as part of Operation Deep Freeze, set up a base, today known as McMurdo Station, on Ross Island.

The New Zealand Antarctic Society, first established in 1933, was a vociferous advocate of New Zealand playing a leading role in the Ross Dependency. It welcomed Fuchs' idea of a trans-Antarctic expedition and lobbied the New Zealand government to support it.

Coincidentally, pressure was being brought to bear on the New Zealand government of the day from another quarter. The International Geophysical Year of 1957 was fast approaching, and a base in the Ross Dependency would greatly enhance New Zealand's scientific contribution to this global undertaking. There had been only two previous International Geophysical Years (then called International Polar Years); the first in 1882–83 and the second, fifty years later, in 1932–33. The idea behind these events was to coordinate, encourage and share international knowledge, expeditions and research into the polar regions, with the principal areas of interest including meteorology, ionospherics, physics, geomagnetism and the aurora. There was comparatively much less understood about Antarctica than the Arctic, due to its geographical isolation from the more populous northern hemisphere. Accordingly, New Zealand was in an ideal location to facilitate research in the Ross Sea area.

PREPARATIONS

The most obvious difficulty with any undertaking in Antarctica is its inaccessibility. Finally, in May 1955, the New Zealand government announced that it would grant £50,000 in support of the New Zealand role in the TAE. Any further funds that were required would have to be raised from the public. An administrative organisation, the Ross Sea Committee of the TAE, was set up to manage New Zealand's participation in the expedition. A month later, in June 1955, the Ross Sea Committee formally offered Ed the leadership of the New Zealand party of the TAE.

Later that year the government also announced that it would fund the full cost of New Zealand's International Geophysical Year (IGY) programme in Antarctica. Taking a practical and cooperative approach, the Ross Sea and IGY committees agreed that only one Antarctic base was necessary and that they would share it. The base was to be sited in McMurdo Sound and would be completed in time to support Fuchs' crossing of Antarctica, planned for the 1957–58 Antarctic summer, and also the IGY which was scheduled to begin on 1 July 1957.

Any programme in the Antarctic needs to take into account both the forbidding Southern Ocean, which surrounds it, and more particularly the continent's harsh climate. The Antarctic summer is brief. The continent's extreme temperatures combine with relentless winds, and months of complete darkness. Consequently, although the TAE and IGY were not due to commence until 1957, it was necessary to send advance parties of men south in the summer of 1955–56 to lay the groundwork for the following year.

PARTIES

The first advance party, which included Fuchs and Hillary, set sail for the Weddell Sea, on the South American side of Antarctica, to select a site for Shackleton Base.

The second advance party, consisting of three of the New Zealand party, travelled to McMurdo Sound with the American Deep Freeze programme. They were charged with investigating suitable sites on which to build New Zealand's Scott Base and, of equal importance to the TAE, potentially accessible routes up on to the Polar Plateau.

A third advance party, consisting of just one man, travelled into Australian Antarctic territory. Harry Ayres, a New Zealand mountain guide of formidable experience, temporarily joined the Australian National Antarctic Research Expedition with the primary objective of gaining experience in the training and use of husky dogs.

WEDDELL SEA ADVANCE PARTY

Ed and Bob Miller, the deputy leader of the New Zealand party of the TAE, arrived in Uruguay on 7 December 1955 and boarded *Theron*, a 900-ton Canadian sealer. Fuchs was already on board, having set sail three weeks earlier from London. Two other New Zealanders were also on board: Ed's great friend, Everest companion and fellow mountaineer, George Lowe, and Squadron Leader John Claydon.

ANTARCTICA

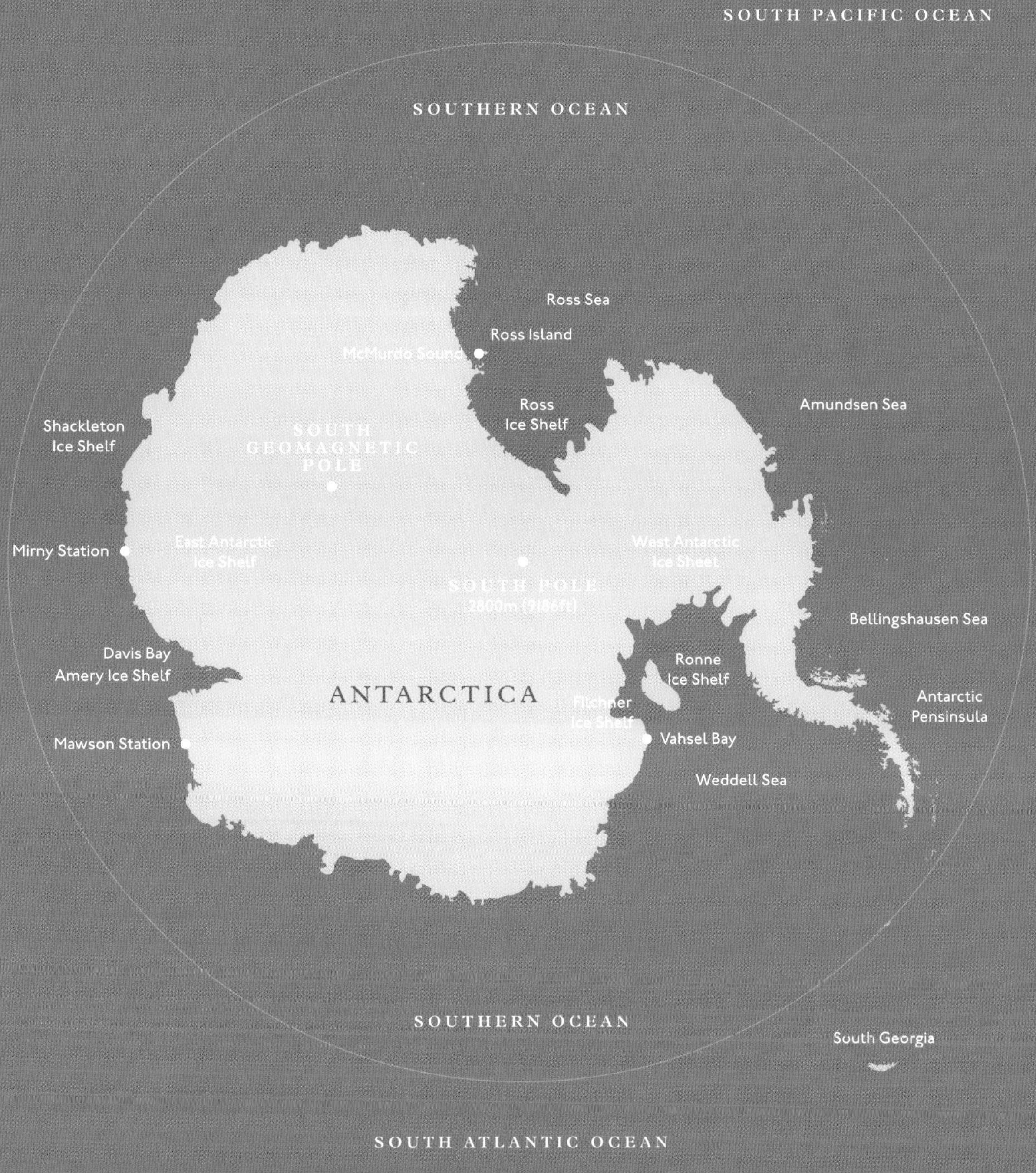

SOUTH PACIFIC OCEAN

SOUTHERN OCEAN

Ross Sea

Ross Island

McMurdo Sound

Amundsen Sea

Ross
Ice Shelf

Shackleton
Ice Shelf

SOUTH
GEOMAGNETIC
POLE

West Antarctic
Ice Sheet

Mirny Station

East Antarctic
Ice Shelf

SOUTH POLE
2800m (9186ft)

Bellingshausen Sea

Davis Bay
Amery Ice Shelf

Ronne
Ice Shelf

Antarctic
Pensinsula

ANTARCTICA

Filchner
Ice Shelf

Mawson Station

Vahsel Bay

Weddell Sea

SOUTHERN OCEAN

South Georgia

SOUTH ATLANTIC OCEAN

Lowe was to be a member of Fuchs' TAE crossing party, and Claydon the chief pilot of Hillary's team.

Theron set off, stopping for a brief few days at South Georgia, a mountainous, stormy and beautiful island and the last, sparsely inhabited settlement before the empty south. It was the setting for Shackleton's final desperate dash to raise help for the remainder of his men marooned on desolate Elephant Island. *Theron* left South Georgia on 20 December, and the island was barely out of sight before the first icebergs were spotted.

Notoriously difficult to penetrate in summer, and impossible in winter, the Weddell Sea is home to vast quantities of sea ice, endlessly clashing and separating, carried around ceaselessly on a mighty carousel of ocean currents. The aim was to pick a route through the pack ice as far south as possible

and, hopefully, reach the Filchner Ice Shelf. This was the same objective that Shackleton had sought, with disastrous consequences, forty years earlier.

The conventional route was to head south through the pack ice on the eastern side of the Weddell Sea. There was usually a fickle channel of open water immediately adjacent to the Caird Coast. Fuchs, however, was of the view that there were two areas of floating ice that rotated independently of each other. In the middle of these great crushing behemoths, he believed, would be a relatively ice-free area that would lead them straight down to Vahsel Bay. Despite the reluctance of *Theron*'s captain, Fuchs insisted that the ship follow this route. As time would soon tell, this was a significant mistake.

The Canadian sealer *Theron* is freed
from surrounding ice.

The ship made poor progress for over four weeks. Often it was caught in the pack ice, like a fly in a web, only to be released and then caught again. Each time it became stuck, *Theron* would be swept along at the mercy of the currents and make no headway south. A ship trapped by ice is in grave danger. Rather like the gathering momentum of an unruly crowd, pressure builds up through the competing pressures of sea ice and ocean currents. Caught in the wrong spot, a ship will be crushed.

Finally, Fuchs called for assistance. HMS *Protector*, a 4000-ton British ice patrol vessel that was near Port Lockroy on the Antarctic Peninsula, travelled to the edge of the sea ice, 80 kilometres away from *Theron*, to be ready to provide help. This was not, in the end, required, but the ship's presence provided reassurance. *Theron*'s captain managed to ease his vessel onward and break free of the pack ice, finally reaching *Protector*. A whaler was sent over from *Protector* to collect the men on *Theron* and, gratefully accepting an invitation to board the larger ship, the men excitedly climbed up a swaying 6-metre rope ladder to her deck, keen to have a break from the relatively small confines of their Canadian sealer. When it was Ed's turn to negotiate the ladder, a sailor above called out, 'Hold tight, sir; think you can manage it?' Another sailor quickly responded, 'He's all right. Climbed Everest, didn't he?'[2]

It was now 24 January 1956 and over a month since they had entered the Weddell Sea. Parting from HMS *Protector*, after enjoying dinner and a convivial evening, they set a course for the usual route over to the east and south down the Caird Coast. The vessel now managed to make significant progress. By 29 January they were at Vahsel Bay, at the eastern end of the Filchner Ice Shelf. Fuchs chose a site 45 kilometres west, where the Filchner Ice Shelf sloped down to meet the sea ice, to dock and unload supplies. At the top of the steep slope, about 1.5 kilometres from the sea and perched on top of 400 metres of floating ice, was the site that Fuchs chose for Shackleton Base.

The summer was rapidly ending. The men worked frantically to unload all of the building materials, food, fuel and vehicles on to the ice edge. Only a week after their arrival, and with many of the supplies not yet transported up to

the base, *Theron* was forced to depart. A massive amount of pack ice was bearing down on them from the north, and if the vessel became trapped there would be no escape until the following summer.

Due to the lateness of their arrival, there had been no time to begin building Shackleton Base. Eight men were left behind, under the leadership of Ken Blaiklock, and their only shelter consisted of some tents and a packing case that had contained the Sno-Cat, an enormous specialised ice vehicle. This was supposed to serve as an emergency shelter only but, as things turned out, the men would be forced to use it as their quarters for the entire Antarctic winter.

Although they had succeeded in reaching the southernmost part of the Weddell Sea, and in delivering the personnel and supplies, Ed knew that the job had not been well done: 'As we drew away from the ice edge the … men left behind looked a lonely and forlorn group, and I doubt if there was anybody on board who didn't feel that we could have done more for them. Few parties have been deposited in the Antarctic so late in the season with so much to do.'[3]

For Ed, the experience highlighted the value of meticulous planning. He took many lessons from this trip and used them to great effect when it was his turn, this time in the Ross Sea, to find and establish Scott Base. He was determined that his own expedition members would never be left in such a precarious predicament.

ROSS SEA ADVANCE PARTY

On the same day that Ed was sailing south from South Georgia, three members of the New Zealand party arrived at Ross Island, on the Ross Sea side of Antarctica. They were there courtesy of the US Navy's Operation Deep Freeze 1, the first of the Deep Freeze missions, also established under the impetus of the upcoming 1957–58 International Geophysical Year.

Dr Trevor Hatherton, an English physicist, was the leader of the New Zealand IGY party. With him was Bernie Gunn, a geologist and mountaineer. Both these men would winter over the following year as members of the New Zealand party. The third member was Lieutenant-Commander Bill Smith of the New Zealand Navy. The three men

Hut Point, Ross Island, with a view to Mount
Discovery and Brown Peninsula (right).

ROSS ISLAND

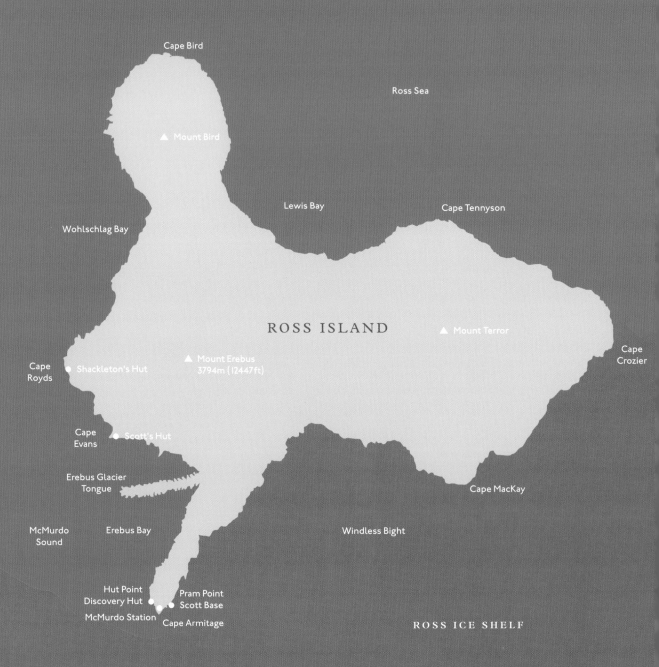

Cape Bird

Ross Sea

▲ Mount Bird

Lewis Bay

Cape Tennyson

Wohlschlag Bay

ROSS ISLAND

▲ Mount Terror

Cape Crozier

Cape
Royds ● Shackleton's Hut

▲ Mount Erebus
3794m (12447ft)

Cape
Evans ● Scott's Hut

Erebus Glacier
Tongue

Cape MacKay

McMurdo
Sound

Erebus Bay

Windless Bight

Hut Point
Discovery Hut ● ● Pram Point
Scott Base

McMurdo Station ●

Cape Armitage

ROSS ICE SHELF

MCMURDO
ICE SHELF

were to work together and pool their experience in preparation for the New Zealand party's arrival the following summer.

Hatherton, as well as assessing sites for building Scott Base, was interested in gathering information about the Americans' IGY plans as part of his mandate to plan and implement significant polar research in preparation for leading the IGY party. Gunn was tasked with assessing access to suitable sites for the building of Scott Base. These would need to have suitable ground conditions, be accessible to landing aircraft and be in the proximity of practical routes, via enormous glaciers, up on to the Polar Plateau. Smith's role was to take aerial photographs of the McMurdo Sound area, to learn as much as practicable about the working conditions, clothing and equipment required to work in the polar conditions, and to gain valuable information on sites for offloading stores the following season.

The immensely important task of choosing a site for building Scott Base was to be key. To further their assessment, Hatherton and Smith, accompanied by Bill Hartigan, an American filmmaker from NBC, set off on a sledging journey around the McMurdo Sound coast. The Americans' Deep Freeze programme provided them with US military one-man hauling sledges and flew them to the western side of the sound to start their trip. The sledging journey lasted five days and the men covered nearly 160 kilometres.

Various sites for Scott Base were considered, including Taylor Valley, Butter Point, Cape Chocolate and the Dailcy Islands. The most promising of these was Butter Point. It had been named by Captain Scott during his 1901–04 expedition, after one of his men left a tin of butter there in the hope of using it to fry up fresh seal meat. It had the virtues of access by sea, access by air via a landing strip on the sea ice in the early season and on the Ferrar Glacier later in the season, and an overland route up the nearby glacier on to the Polar Plateau.

As expected, the group's travel was onerous and certainly not comfortable. On one occasion, the men were suffering with very wet socks and feet. Perhaps indicating that his skills lay in creative pursuits other than mountaineering,

Hartigan, as recalled by Hatherton, came up with a novel solution: 'Bill Hartigan suggested that we heat our wet socks in a dry billy. Smithie experimented (with a pair of my socks, naturally) and the tent reeks with the odour of burnt wool.' Hatherton, ever the scientist, drily recorded that 'the experiment was unsuccessful'.[4]

On reaching Hut Point, at the southern end of McMurdo Sound, the men were dissuaded from seriously considering it as a site for the base due to the long distance between the point and the supply ships waiting beyond the line of pack ice, further north in the sound.

Attention turned to the possible routes on to the Polar Plateau. It was hoped that the Ferrar Glacier would provide the answer, so Hatherton, Gunn and Smith decided to undertake a sledging journey up the glacier. Again they received help from the Americans, who flew them about 16 kilometres up the glacier and provided them with rations to last eleven days. Hauling the sledges was hard work as the Americans tended to rely on mechanical transport and had very little in the way of lightweight food rations to donate to the cause. Consequently, the New Zealand contingent loaded their sleds with over 125 kilograms of tinned food alone.[5]

In spite of the heavy loads, the men hauled their way up the glacier for another 80 kilometres or so and succeeded in reaching the Polar Plateau after five days. In their report of the journey, the men expressed confidence in the Ferrar as an accessible route between the Plateau and the Ross Sea. They also noted that there appeared to be several potentially suitable base sites on its lower reaches.

Importantly, Gunn had the opportunity to join a flight to photograph other possible routes, including the Koettlitz, Skelton, Mulock and Shackleton glaciers. The most promising seemed to be the Skelton Glacier, and Gunn compiled valuable information on a possible approach route.

After the sledging journeys and aerial reconnaissance had been carried out, and following discussions with Gunn and Smith, Hatherton made a list of six potential sites for a New Zealand Scott Base.[6] Pram Point, where Scott Base was eventually built in January 1957, was not one of them.

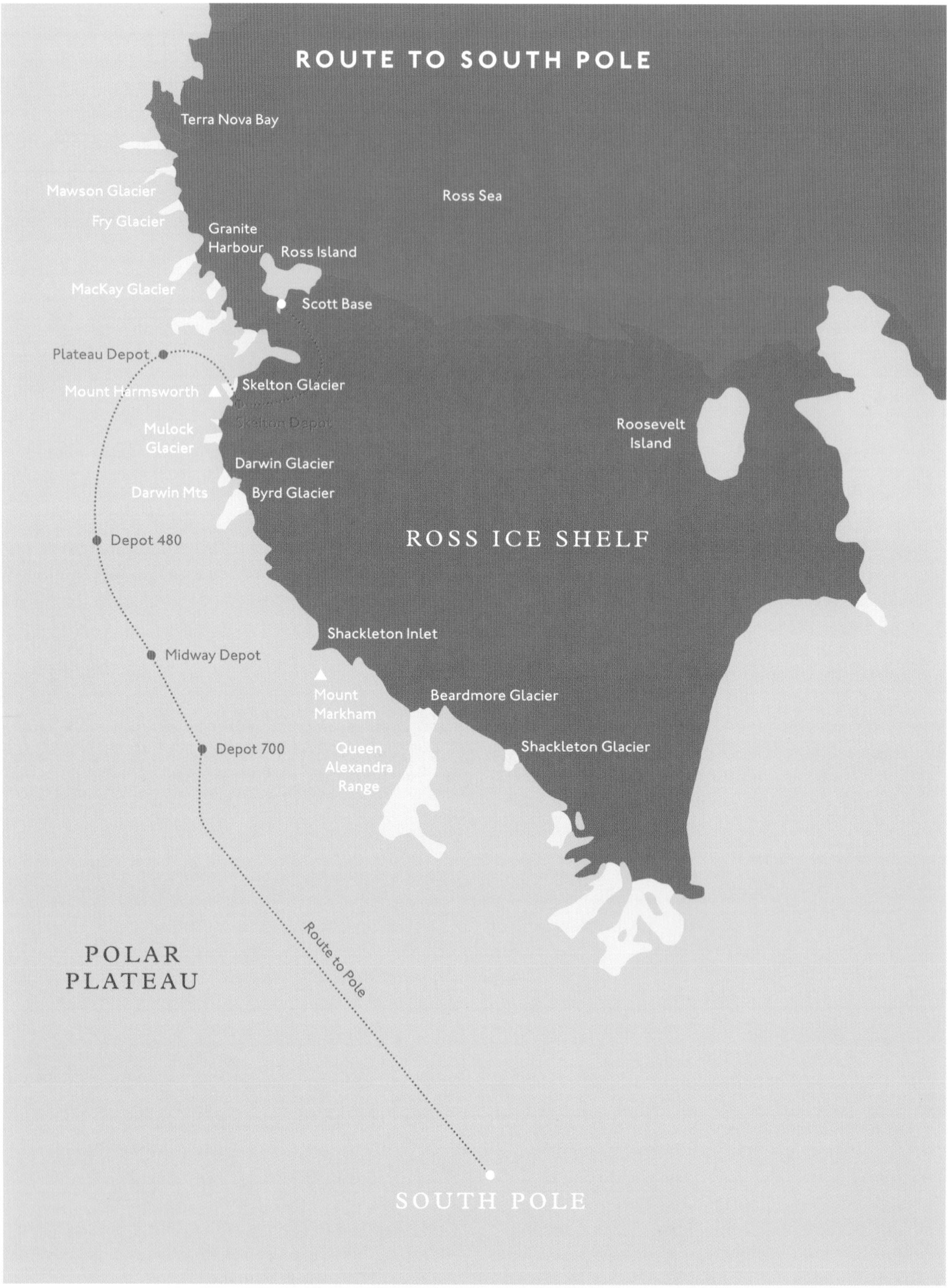

ROUTE TO SOUTH POLE

Terra Nova Bay

Ross Sea

Mawson Glacier

Fry Glacier

Granite
Harbour

Ross Island

MacKay Glacier

Scott Base

Plateau Depot

Skelton Glacier

Mount Harmsworth

Roosevelt
Island

Skelton Depot

Mulock
Glacier

Darwin Glacier

Darwin Mts

Byrd Glacier

ROSS ICE SHELF

Depot 480

Shackleton Inlet

Midway Depot

Mount
Markham

Beardmore Glacier

Depot 700

Shackleton Glacier

Queen
Alexandra
Range

POLAR
PLATEAU

Route to Pole

SOUTH POLE

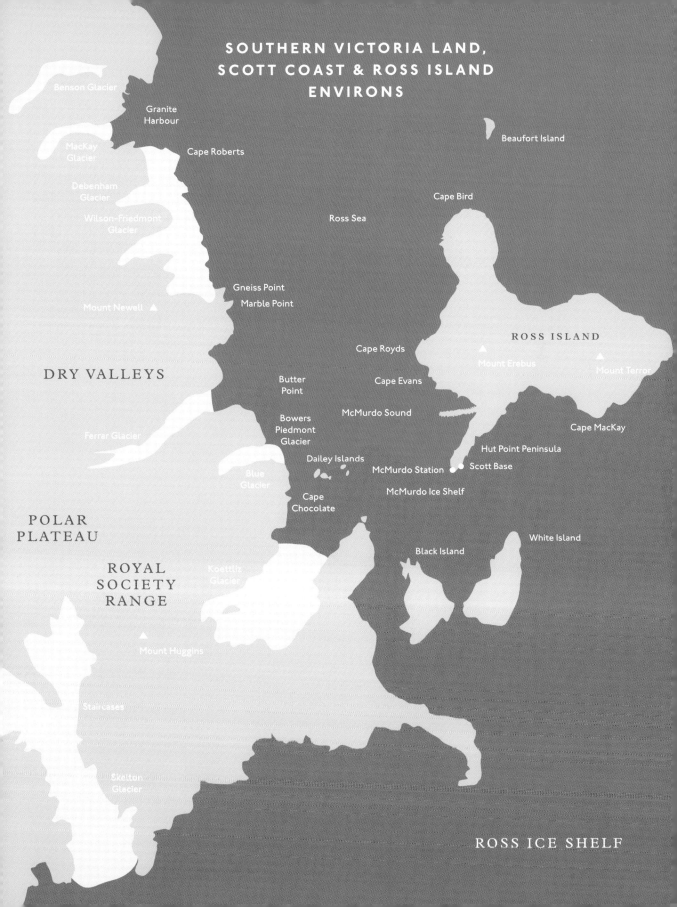

SOUTHERN VICTORIA LAND,
SCOTT COAST & ROSS ISLAND
ENVIRONS

Benson Glacier

Granite
Harbour

Beaufort Island

MacKay
Glacier

Cape Roberts

Debenham
Glacier

Cape Bird

Wilson-Friedmont
Glacier

Ross Sea

Gneiss Point

Marble Point

ROSS ISLAND

Mount Newell ▲

Cape Royds

Mount Erebus ▲

▲ Mount Terror

DRY VALLEYS

Cape Evans

Butter
Point

McMurdo Sound

Ferrar Glacier

Bowers
Piedmont
Glacier

Cape MacKay

Dailey Islands

Hut Point Peninsula

McMurdo Station

Scott Base

Blue
Glacier

McMurdo Ice Shelf

Cape
Chocolate

POLAR
PLATEAU

White Island

ROYAL
SOCIETY
RANGE

Black Island

Koettlitz
Glacier

▲

Mount Huggins

Staircases

Skelton
Glacier

ROSS ICE SHELF

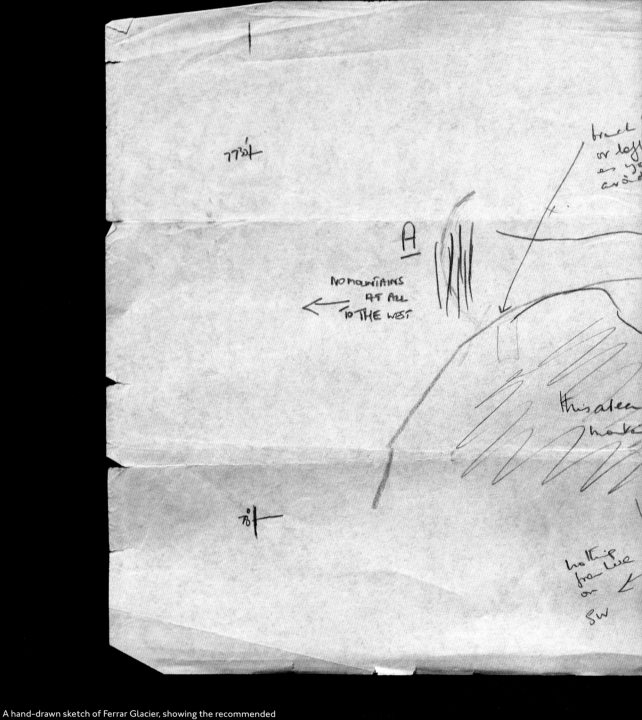

A hand-drawn sketch of Ferrar Glacier, showing the recommended route of travel to avoid crevassed areas during the Ross Sea Advance Party's exploratory journey in January 1956. This comes from Trevor Hatherton's personal effects. He credited it as a tracing of a BAE (British Antarctic Expedition 1910–13) chart.

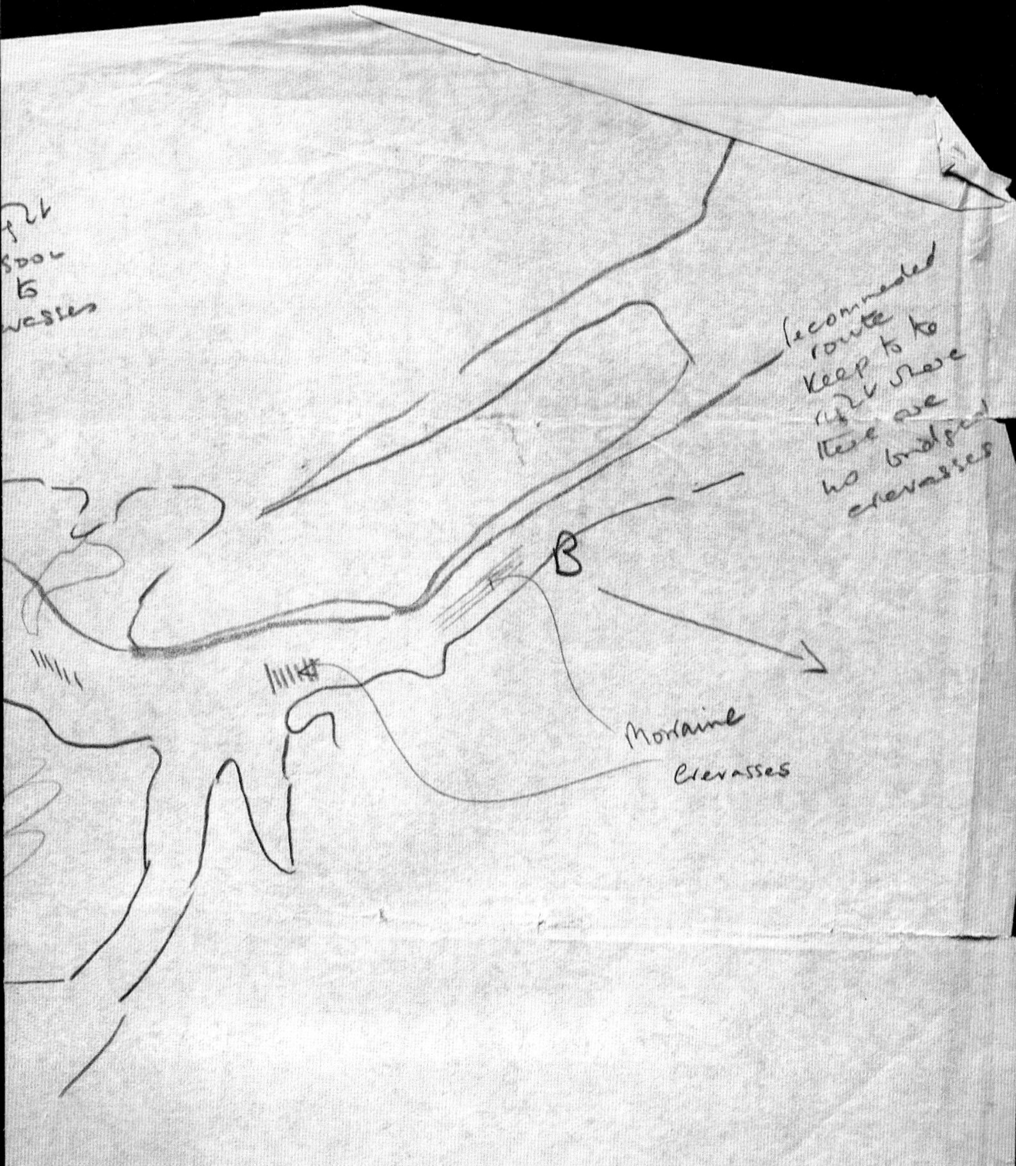

recommended route to keep to right where there are no bridged crevasses

B

Morraine
Crevasses

Graeipot BAE chot.

'Phil disappeared down crevasses, highly exciting ...once again the rope saved the day.'

HARRY AYRES

Making up an advance party of one, Harry Ayres travelled south to the Australian Antarctic coastline on MV *Kista Dan*, a ship built for navigating the ice, with the Australian National Antarctic Research Expedition (ANARE). Ayres was the second man to be chosen for the New Zealand party, after Ed, a reflection of the standing in which his immense mountaineering experience and expertise was held. Ayres was Hillary's climbing mentor in his early days, and had originally been selected as the third New Zealander for the Everest attempt in 1953. The invitation was later revoked in view of his status as a professional guide, but he was not to be denied this Antarctic adventure.

In addition to obtaining experience in an Antarctic summer, Ayres was tasked by the Ross Sea Committee with collecting thirty husky dogs which had been promised to New Zealand by the Australians. The Australians, for their part, wished to take advantage of his mountaineering skills.

Landing at Davis Bay on 7 January 1956, Ayres saved the life of both the ANARE leader Philip Law and a companion. They were climbing up a cliff of ice that rose for a sheer 38 metres out of the freezing ocean. Three-quarters of the way up, with the men roped together and Ayres in the lead, the trailing man cried out and fell, dragging Law with him. Ayres, hearing the cry, averted certain disaster by digging in his axe and making a few quick coils in the climbing rope, thereby taking the weight of the two dangling men. In his rather dry manner, Ayres recorded the event in his diary:

> Phil Law asked me if I could climb up the cliff on to the shelf. I roped he and one other up and did so. Took two hours or more, step-cutting required for crampons. Phil disappeared down crevasses, highly exciting day. He and Bill had good slip on slope above water, but once again the rope saved the day. I guess I needed a second guide, as it stands my prestige is high right now.[7]

When talking about the incident later, Ayres' explanation for his actions was simple: 'We were right over the sea. I can't swim, and was certainly not planning to learn then.'[8]

The expedition continued along the coast, stopping to visit the Russians who were establishing Mirny Station on Haswell Island, and were in the midst of unloading their ship and constructing huts. It was useful for Ayres to observe the types of vehicles they were using and their techniques for sledge-hauling over sea ice to the base. A couple of days were spent with the Russians, and a considerable quantity of vodka was consumed amidst much conviviality. The day after the first night's socialising, Ayres and his Australian colleagues sought the Russians' company once more: 'they were suffering hang-overs so we were then asked to partake of vodka (a new kind of kerosene) ... Alexi sang and played guitar very well, then insisted we ... have more vodka.'[9]

Harry Ayres in Antarctica.

Departing from the Russian base the next day, Ayres noted in his diary that a number of the Australians 'have turned up with Russian hats and various articles of clothing draped all over and it is difficult to tell whether they are Aussie or Russian'.[10]

No doubt all had a delightful time with the Russians but, as it was the height of the Cold War in 1956, the men were directed to write a report after their visit to Mirny. Not only was the visit newsworthy when Ayres returned to New Zealand, but he also received a visit from government bureaucrats seeking information about his time with the Russians.[11]

Kista Dan eventually reached the Australian Antarctic station of Mawson on 17 February 1956. Two weeks were spent there, during which time the Australians were busy building prefabricated huts and aircraft hangars. The thirty dogs that Ayres was to collect had been reduced in number to just over twenty adult dogs and five puppies, but they were wonderfully large and powerful, heavily coated and perfect for the job ahead.

Harry Ayres prepares for adventure.

THE

ADVENTURE

BEGINS

THREE

FOLLOWING PAGE: The night sky over Antarctica.

With the return of the advance parties it was time to prepare for the next stage of the expedition. There were twenty-two positions available with the New Zealand party, and an astounding 665 men responded to the call for applications. There were thirteen nationalities among the applicants, ranging in age from 15 to 59, and over fifty occupations.

The successful men would be expected to remain for a year in Antarctica and, importantly, would be part of a small team over the long, dark Antarctic winter. Those with the necessary skills would be men with experience as mechanics, mountaineers, surveyors, cooks, pilots, radio operators, geologists, doctors, dog experts, technicians and scientists. Of the twenty-two selected, five were scientists or technicians, with varying polar research objectives, as part of the government's IGY commitment. Hillary decided to add one more man, Murray Douglas, a mountaineer and summer team member, to the wintering party.

Two British members were included in the New Zealand party by Fuchs. They were medical officer George Marsh and surveyor Richard Brooke. Both had experience driving dogs. Fuchs also included two New Zealanders in his own TAE party, pilot Gordon Haslop and Hillary's good friend George Lowe. Lowe went on to make the continental crossing with Fuchs as the official photographer. Fuchs also included an Australian and a South African in his team.

'Antarctica might
as well have been on
the moon as far as
I was concerned.'

SCOTT BASE ARCHITECT
FRANK PONDER

The New Zealand party also required nearly thirty more men to assist with the initial building of Scott Base, setting up of the IGY programme, management, press reporting and cinematography. This group of men would depart from Antarctica before winter, in late February 1957.

Momentum grew in New Zealand. Huge amounts of time, planning and resources were required to prepare for the expedition. Not only was a new site to be confirmed and the base designed and constructed, with all the considerations of safety, comfort, food and fuel for nearly two dozen men, but scientific endeavours also needed to be supported and organised. Then there were sixty dogs to house, feed and exercise (extras had been added to Ayres' group, sourced from Auckland Zoo and from Greenland). On top of all that were the logistical dilemmas posed by proving a route from sea level up to the Polar Plateau and, once there, stocking food and fuel depots for Fuchs' TAE crossing party.

Overshadowing events was the fact that the New Zealand party had insufficient funds. The government's grant, and its purchase of the expedition vessel for the New Zealand Navy, was not enough to cover the considerable costs of the venture, and much time was spent in public fundraising. The aim was to raise another £100,000, and despite a prevailing view among the public that the government should be footing the entire bill,[1] by dint of hard work and perseverance over £50,000 was added to the fund.

DESIGNING SCOTT BASE

'Antarctica might as well have been on the moon as far as I was concerned.'[2] With those words the New Zealand Ministry of Works architect Frank Ponder described the assignment he faced to build a base in Antarctica. In less than a year it was necessary to design, transport, build and occupy the base. In exasperation he later recalled that 'there were no precedents!'[3] He noted, 'There was nowhere to turn for help and now they expected me to design a base there and organise its construction in less than a year! Impossible!'[4] With assistance, he delivered the impossible, later praising his 'enthusiastic' architectural draughtsman Ron Mitchell, and Randal Heke, whom he appointed to head the construction team.

Ponder's previous experience with prefabricated buildings persuaded him that they would fit the brief. As it turned out, the Australians were also using this method in the Antarctic and they freely shared their experience. Large prefabricated insulated panels, bolted together, had the advantages of quicker construction and better insulation compared with the tried and tested wooden buildings with precut timber that had been used in the Antarctic for half a century. The downside was the additional cost.

Fuchs and Hillary were not impressed. In a cable Hillary (in London) sent to the Ross Sea Committee, he wrote:

> Fuchs and self appalled at increased cost and luxury of new hut plan. Strongly recommend deferring of placing of orders until my return… We cannot afford and do not require American hotel comfort and sleeping area or elaborate safety precautions.[5]

Less than a week later Hillary received the response that the Ross Sea Committee had considered his views but would proceed with the prefabricated panelled hut plan. The committee noted that the base must also cater for the IGY party, that the IGY committee would be willing to bear some of the cost, and that Scott Base would be of more permanent character than the British TAE Shackleton Base. It was a good decision.

As yet, no final decision had been made as to exactly where in the McMurdo Sound area of the Ross Sea the base would be located. With this in mind, Ponder designed it to be successfully built regardless of whether the foundation was rock, permafrost or ice.

THE JOURNEY SOUTH

As 1956 drew to an end, all the members of the New Zealand party travelled down to Antarctica by sea. The majority, including Ed, were on HMNZS *Endeavour*. Others were on the American ships USS *Glacier* (sixteen men) and USS *Private John R. Towle* (three men and much equipment). The Americans were to prove hugely helpful to the New Zealand party, assisting in innumerable ways, and their kindness and generosity were to be defining factors in the success of the expedition.

HMNZS *Endeavour* and USS *Private John R. Towle*
moored in ice alongside one another.

There was an inauspicious start, however, when as they were leaving Lyttelton Harbour the wing of the Auster aircraft, which overhung the stern, clipped another ship, causing damage to the wing. But as *Endeavour* pulled away from Bluff in late December 1956, their great adventure was finally under way. Ed reflected that it was with mixed feelings that many of them said goodbye to the New Zealand mainland:

> A large proportion of the wintering party had wives and young children so our partings from these were in more regretful vein. In many ways the tasks our wives faced were more difficult than ours—they had all the work and the worry without the compensations of excitement and adventure. I think many of us had qualms of conscience at the thought of leaving them to battle along on their own for the next fifteen or sixteen months.[6]

Two New Zealand frigates escorted *Endeavour* to the edge of the pack ice and, this being the Southern Ocean, the passage was not without its challenges of weather and ice conditions. There was, however, time to celebrate the arrival of 1957, which Bob Miller did with some gusto:

> A party warmed up towards midnight with good cheer. We had the CPO's [Chief Petty Officers] and POs [Petty Officers] into our mess…The harmonica band Harry Ayres, Murray Ellis and myself has now become an institution.[7]

New Year's Day was unpleasant, especially for those nursing sore heads from the celebrations the evening before:

> A very heavy swell running. By 6.30 out of pack and in a raging sea. Full storm. Most did not get very far from bunks. A violent crashing in mess about 7 am. Took in and helped to straighten things out and like most others had retired to bed with thoughts of an 'old English folk song' with which we had charmed others at 4 am. We had played 'On Ilkla Moor Baht 'at' to Yorkshire man Hatherton [leader of the IGY party] at 4.15 am. At midday I filmed from bridge waves crashing over the bars. Earlier seas had tumbled the for'ard dog crates backwards, but Richard Brooke in particular was responsible for salvage. One dog loose. It is a sailor's day.[8]

Bob Miller's sledging compass (left) and his brass
pocket compass with belt loop and fastening latch
(above), both used on the expedition.

At least one of Miller's fellow carousers, Harry Ayres, lay unmoving in his bunk wondering what he had got himself into:

> When I feel ill like this I can't imagine why I ever wanted to come as life on one of these things is hell in rough seas. It would be so pleasant back at Heather Place even with the long grass.[9]

The rough conditions continued for three days causing general discomfort and, on the third day, havoc when a huge wave broke on to the deck and smashed four of the dog crates. The men scrambled to grab the dogs before they were washed overboard. Two of the dogs, Blue and Skinny, were part of the team looked after by Ayres. Skinny was to become a great favourite of Ayres and destined to play a leading role in an exciting, albeit tragic, encounter with a crevasse.

On 4 January 1957, with assistance from USS *Glacier* in breaking a path through the pack ice, *Endeavour* steamed into McMurdo Sound. It is a beautiful place. The surface of the ocean is covered in an ever-changing jigsaw of ice. To the west are the Trans-Antarctic Mountains, a line of alpine giants with huge glaciers cascading down from great heights. To the east is Ross Island, permanently attached to the Antarctic mainland by the Ross Ice Shelf which runs along its southern shores.

Just 80 kilometres across and one and a half times the size of Stewart Island, Ross Island is home to the world's southernmost active volcano, Mount Erebus. With plumes of smoke often rising from its crater, it dominates the island, along with another peak, Mt Terror. Erebus and Terror were named after the two ships that, under the command of the British naval officer James Clark Ross, first entered this landscape. It is astounding that in 1841, when the ink was just drying on New Zealand's Treaty of Waitangi, this remote and treacherous area was being mapped. Between the two mountains is Terra Nova, named after one of Captain Robert Falcon Scott's ships, best-known as part of his last, fatal expedition in 1910–13.

THE SEARCH FOR A BASE SITE

As a result of the Ross Sea advance party's report on possible sites for Scott Base, the expectation was that Butter Point, at the foot of the Ferrar Glacier, would be suitable. This expectation was severely challenged as soon as Ed arrived in McMurdo Sound. Not only was the sea ice preventing *Endeavour* from getting any closer than 19 kilometres but the weather was so mild that huge melt pools were appearing in the ice,[10] making it very dangerous to traverse. Guyon Warren, a New Zealand party geologist who had arrived on the USS *Private John R. Towle*, was similarly unimpressed by Butter Point when flown there by helicopter on Christmas Day 1956:

> The first impression for what it's worth is a bit disappointing. We will be on a sloping moraine terrace, a few hundred feet quite steeply above the Ferrar which here looks just like any other area of flat uninteresting bay ice … At the moment it is a soft mushy mess, or at least it is at the bottom where we stopped. We had heard earlier that Butter Point was ice-free but whoever saw this weren't at this Butter Point because there is a huge area of bay ice as far as you can see from 50 feet up.[11]

Ed, equally concerned about sea access to the site, was not quite so pessimistic about the area's qualities. The shingle beach was roomy enough for huts and aerials,[12] and he considered that it was worth a bit more effort before abandoning the location. Setting off with four tractors towing seven sledges, and three dog teams, a route was picked through the rough, broken sea ice from *Endeavour* to within a mile of Butter Point. The exercise was arduous and dangerous and, ultimately, proved to Ed that the site was highly inadequate.

The Americans were by now settled into their base, on the other side of McMurdo Sound, at Hut Point on Ross Island. Several dozen men had already wintered over there and they had built a runway on the sea ice nearby. The Americans operating in Antarctica were under the command of Rear Admiral George Dufek. In the New Zealand party's official account Dufek was described as 'a generous and warm-hearted friend to those associated with the New Zealand Party and to the TAE in general'.[13]

It is not overstating things to say that the American support was the defining factor in the successful establishment of Scott Base and the tractor journey to the South Pole. Without their assistance the expedition's outcome would have been very different. Central to this support was Dufek. While he was fifteen years Hillary's senior, he was very media savvy and knew how positive the association with Everest's conqueror would be. Not only that, 'he took a liking to Ed and would do anything for him'.[14] Dufek did all in his power to help throughout the expedition.

Dufek suggested that he would be pleased to have the New Zealanders as neighbours on Ross Island, and Ed resolved to investigate an area called Pram Point, just slightly to the southeast of Hut Point.

Hillary and Miller flew to Pram Point at the first available opportunity on an American helicopter. The point is on the southern tip of Ross Island, looking south over the Ross Ice Shelf; it is named after the small Norwegian-style dinghy, or pram, that the men of Captain Scott's first expedition used to traverse the late summer's ice-free water. First impressions of the site were positive. It was spacious and on solid rock. There was plenty of room for buildings and radio antennae. The nearby Weddell seal rookery would provide interest to the IGY biologist and food for the dogs. Miller was 'delighted' with the site,[15] and Ed was sold:

> The more we walked around Pram Point the more my interest and enthusiasm grew. It was a very pleasant spot and the views were magnificent. To the north of us were the great volcanoes Erebus and Terror. To the south stretched the Ross Ice Shelf broken only by the low outlines of White and Black Islands. And to the west were the lovely mountains of Victoria Land. It had all the advantages of close proximity to the American base and yet was still fresh and untouched … so without much ado I decided that this was the site for Scott Base.[16]

This was a monumental, and unexpected, change to the New Zealand party's plans—Pram Point was never considered as an option in the advance party's report. Subject only to proving the route from the ship with a Ferguson tractor, which they did immediately, this was going to be the new

Scott Base site. As Guyon Warren recorded in his diary, Ed had 'decided to make what is a colossal change in plans with about as much concern as if he was choosing which tie to wear. The fact that he will have to start virtually from scratch again with planning the whole operation, worries him not a scrap.'[17]

Soon after, a large American bulldozer was making its way across the gap between Hut Point and Pram Point to flatten the building site.

Sir Edmund Hillary (left) and Rear Admiral George Dufek at Scott Base in 1957.

OFFLOADING CARGO

Before the construction could begin it was necessary to unload the materials from the ships. Ordinarily this might not be much of an issue, but as *Endeavour* and *Towle* were ten or so miles away and the only way to transport the cargo to the site was by hauling it over temperamental sea ice, the task became very much more difficult. Hillary and Miller, each driving a tractor and pulling a sledge, set up a route. It took them three hours to drive one way, which was not very encouraging, but a great deal better than if the site had been at Butter Point. In any event, as the sea ice progressively retreated in the summer temperatures, the distance would become shorter.

By 12 January 1957, sledge-load after sledge-load began to arrive at the bulldozed base site. It was a major job transporting the roughly

Ed Hillary drives a tractor and stores away from the
side of HMNZS *Endeavour* while Trevor Hatherton
rides the sled.

500 tonnes of stores, fuel and equipment across the sea ice to Pram Point. Hillary was confident that with two US Navy Weasel vehicles (provided by Dufek to the New Zealanders for their use in McMurdo Sound), together with the New Zealand party's five Ferguson tractors, they could complete the task, but they were very long days.

Although they were pleased with the progress they were making, a sad incident reinforced to the men the inherent danger in delivering these many heavily laden sledges across the sea ice. On 14 January news came through to the

New Zealanders that, the evening before, an American working on Operation Deep Freeze had become trapped, and had drowned, when one of their expedition's Weasels had broken through the sea ice. Ed ordered the cabs on their own Weasel vehicles to be removed to allow a quick exit, just in case.

Less than a week after the death of the American, however, the New Zealanders were destined to have their own moment with the dangerously fickle sea ice that was their highway. Hatherton was driving a Weasel, towing two fully laden sledges, with

Hillary and Peter Mulgrew, the New Zealand party's chief radio operator, as passengers. As Hatherton was admiring the beautiful view to the Royal Society Range, Ed commented on how Murray Douglas had suggested the track was becoming quite rotten and that it needed to be rerouted. Suddenly, the back end of the Weasel dipped, the engine stalled and, in spite of Ed's 'hurried injunction to give her more revs', Hatherton was unable to do so:

> [A]nd as the sledge behind crashed through and the Weasel started to slide there was a general abandon ship movement. The rear Greenland sledge was clear but the Maudheim [sledge] was completely in, with the weasel half in and half out, held by the first two notches in its track. Summing up the situation as one that needs power Ed departed for the Base.[18]

A Trans-Antarctic Expedition Weasel lies on its side in a crevasse while two men work to free it.

With the aid of two tractors, another Weasel, strong rope and several men, they managed, after a great deal of time and difficulty, to save the vehicle and the cargo. Afterwards, much care was taken to avoid that particular area of ice and a post-hole digger was used to take soundings all along the track. Hatherton was, no doubt, rather shaken by this experience and recorded in his diary two days later:

> Coined a simile for tractor driving over the dicky route round Cape Armitage—Russian Roulette. Let's call it—Antarctic Roulette.[19]

BUILDING SCOTT BASE

The rapidity with which Scott Base was constructed belies the huge amount of planning, preparation, pre-building and sheer hard graft that went into it. After viewing first-hand the conditions in which Fuchs' men had been left at Shackleton Base the previous summer, Ed had vowed not to repeat that mistake. This resolve was strengthened when word came through that the men at Shackleton Base had been unable to complete their hut before the winter set in and were forced to camp out in their tents, and the empty Sno-Cat crate, in temperatures down to −50°C.

The pre-constructed aluminium panel model that the Ross Sea Committee had settled on had some significant construction and thermal advantages over the traditional prefabricated wooden buildings used by the British polar explorers until that point. The pre-constructed panel frames had a timber frame, an outer layer of aluminium and a core of foam known as ebonite. While nominally fireproof, to be sure, a layer of asbestos was added.

Scott Base itself was to have nine buildings; six were to be connected by covered walkways and the remaining three were detached buildings for scientific study. They were referred to without flourish as Hut A, Hut B, etc.

Prior to being shipped south, the prefabricated Scott Base had been put together in Wellington by a construction team who, after making any necessary modifications, then packed it up and travelled with it down to McMurdo Sound. Once the components were unloaded from the ship and transported to Pram Point, the construction team was able to rebuild the base confidently and efficiently.

The New Zealanders worked around the clock, and after two days the first building, Hut A, had been erected. It would be the hub of the base, comprising the kitchen, mess room, Hillary's office and the radio room. The speed of construction was testament to the planning and design.

The building was strengthened with steel beams and additionally threaded steel rods which passed through the panels and were successively tightened by nuts at each end. The floor of the hut rested on beams, plates and railway sleepers gifted by

New Zealand Railways. It was anchored by a series of steel cables tied to the ground. In view of the climate they were operating in, hot water, instead of cement, was poured into the holes dug in the permafrost to anchor the ends of the guy wires. They froze immediately.

Bob Miller noted in his diary on 14 January 1957:

> A highlight today. Hut A is completed — apart from the titivating and heating installations. A long day's work saw this whole job done — a great credit to Randall Heke and his seven offsiders … Thanks to the careful work we did on the levels of the foundation yesterday everything just slid into place. Nothing was missing or fitting badly. The radio room was the first to be completed.[20]

Less than a week later there was an official opening of Scott Base. It was Sunday, 20 January 1957. Miller recorded in his diary:

> Somewhat a wasted day as far as Base erection goes. Harold Ruegg has wanted to raise a flag and so he did … that's about all except that he brought Admiral Dufek and many other US folks and they had a party which we provided and which the ship enjoyed and so a day is lost but probably ensured friendly relations with Hut Point [US Navy]. Used Scott's old flag pole from Hut Point. Arthur Helm really carried the show …[21]

Robert Falcon Scott's flagpole still stands outside the modern Scott Base.

Three weeks after construction had begun, Scott Base was a living, breathing home for the expedition members:

> Big changes at the base — five huts up now, generators roaring, and most of science's electrical gifts to mankind operating at once in the mess hut. Lights, stove, radios, fans, alarms, the whole works and very nice too. It looks to me as though we are going to be exceptionally comfortable, if not actually bordering on the luxury class.[22]

By mid-February it was time for the ships to leave McMurdo Sound or risk becoming trapped in ice for the winter. After an extremely intense few weeks of activity and base construction, the men were tired. Warren noted in his diary:

> Tonight or early tomorrow Endeavour leaves … At afternoon tea, Ed enquired how many of the rest of us were going down to see them aboard and farewell the ship. A pretty miserable day, and the immediate response was one … After raising with difficulty three or four more to go down with him, Ed suddenly went bolshie, turned very pale, and ordered the whole expedition to turn out, like it or not. It was the first time he had ever needed to do anything like that but I'm convinced it was the right and proper thing and so were most of the others and there were very few grumbles. Ed was quite upset I think.[23]

Hatherton recalled the trip out to the ship: 'at 1700 in Weasel to ice edge. Smooth ride except for last ½ mile when Ed bitched at route chosen. So I stopped and asked him if he would rather get out and walk. He did.'[24]

On the journey back to Scott Base, Ed returned the favour:

> Ed and I were away in a Fergie to the base. Cold southerly blowing. I was on the sledge with no cushioning. Ed went like the bats of hell and I was rather bruised.[25]

The hard-working summer crew, who had been such a vital part of setting up the expedition base, departed on *Endeavour* on 22 February 1957.

ACCESS TO THE POLAR PLATEAU

Pram Point did have one major disadvantage as the site of Scott Base. Butter Point was always preferred due to its proximity to the Ferrar Glacier, which was presumed, at the time, to be the most likely route up to the Polar Plateau. Pram Point's location added another 50 kilometres of travel.

At the same time as Ed was making his decision on the siting of Scott Base, he had sent a group of men — George Marsh, Richard Brooke, Harry Ayres and Murray Ellis — together with three dog teams, to explore a route up the Ferrar.

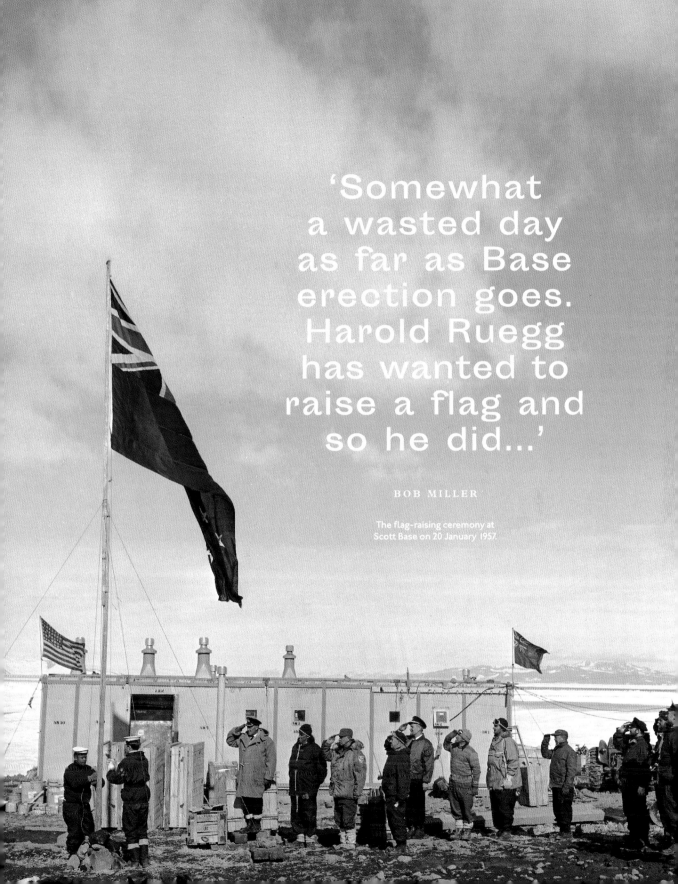

'Somewhat a wasted day as far as Base erection goes. Harold Ruegg has wanted to raise a flag and so he did...'

BOB MILLER

The flag-raising ceremony at Scott Base on 20 January 1957.

Hut A (Hillary's hut), with a view south to White Island and Minna Bluff (right) in the distance.

BELOW: Looking west to Hut A (Hillary's hut), with Observation Hill in the background.

CENTRE AND FACING PAGE: Entrance porches to the hut.

'A highlight today. Hut A is completed—apart from the titivating and heating installations. A long day's work saw this whole job done—a great credit to Randall Heke and his seven offsiders...'

BOB MILLER

FACING PAGE: View into the cold porch and inner porch from the outer porch. The cold porch provided a transition area between the heated interior of Hut A and the uninsulated covered linkway that joined the base buildings.

PAGE 52: Another view into the cold porch from the inner porch, looking towards the original diesel fuel storage unit.

PAGE 53: The original Waterbury heater in the cold porch.

PAGES 54 AND 55: Views from the cold porch looking into the mess room.

The Ross Sea advance party, under Hatherton, had of course managed this the year before, but they had been flown several miles up rather than start the climb at sea level. In mid-January 1957 Marsh reported that access on to the Ferrar was hopeless. The first several miles were rotten masses of melt pools, icy pinnacles and huge ice trenches.[26] This was another disappointment. The previous summer, however, Bernie Gunn had noticed, while on his aerial reconnaissance, that the Skelton Glacier held possibilities for a successful route up to the Polar Plateau. Ed now turned his attention to exploring this option.

On 19 January Marsh, Brooke and Ayres set off again, with the dog teams, but this time Peter Mulgrew, instead of Ellis, joined them as fourth man on a reconnaissance trip across the expansive Ross Ice Shelf to the Skelton Glacier. Unfortunately disaster struck within a few days. The doctor, George Marsh, became alarmingly unwell. Unable to

Aircraft on the Ross Ice Shelf close to the Skelton Depot. This photo was taken later in the Trans-Antarctic Expedition, hence the Sno-Cat vehicle in shot.

make radio contact using the inadequate field radio sets, Brooke and Mulgrew drove their dog teams for 51 kilometres, over seven hours, to raise the alarm. Marsh was airlifted out, eventually diagnosed with diphtheria, and the others recalled to base.

Aware that the summer would rapidly slip away, Ed decided to save time and fly the men and their dogs to the foot of the Skelton Glacier to continue their reconnaissance. He abandoned his cautious advice that the precious aircraft were not to be landed out in the field unless a ground party was able to inspect the landing area. There simply was not time. Wishing to assess the area at the bottom of the Skelton Glacier before airlifting the dog teams there, Ed flew with Brooke in the Beaver aircraft piloted by Claydon. They spied what looked like a reasonable landing area and flew down to land. To their horror, the surface was actually covered with hard ice outcrops, known as sastrugi, some several feet high:

Dog teams successfully forged their way up to the
Polar Plateau in February 1957. In this later photo,
tractor teams lay a depot on the site.

We touched with a tremendous crash—the
snow was as hard as iron—and crash followed
crash as we lurched from one bump to the
next and rocked violently around in our seats.
It really seemed as if we were for it! John had
seen the danger and reacted immediately. He
swept the throttle open and tried to lift the
plane off once more. The propeller clawed at
the air, there were a couple more resounding
crashes, and then to our immense relief, we
floated up to safety.[27]

Clearly this part of the glacier was not suitable for
landing, but they eventually found another area
that was. The dog teams, with Brooke, Ayres,
Ellis and Douglas, were successfully flown in on
28 January. After ten days they made it to the top
of the Skelton Glacier and to the Polar Plateau.
Success!

An attempt to establish a Plateau Depot
while the men were up there and available to
unload the aircraft led to another unpleasant

aerial experience. The New Zealand party had
two planes, a Beaver and an Auster. Despite both
planes landing successfully up on the Polar
Plateau, the Auster had a great deal of difficulty
getting airborne again in the thin, high-altitude
(2400-metre) air. Circling above in the Beaver,
Ed watched with growing horror as Bill Cranfield
struggled at the controls of the Auster:

He went on and on over the plateau, churning
up clouds of powder snow, but not getting
airborne. It was something of a relief when
he finally limped into the air and flew up to
join us. The Auster must have been just about
operating at its limit for takeoff height and
after this we made no more landings on the
plateau with it.[28]

Although the Auster was no longer to be used at
high altitude, the New Zealand party still had the
Beaver and, with relief, the worry about whether
the Polar Plateau depots could be stocked by air
was over.[29]

'He went on
and on over the
plateau, churning
up clouds of powder
snow, but not
getting airborne...'

ED HILLARY

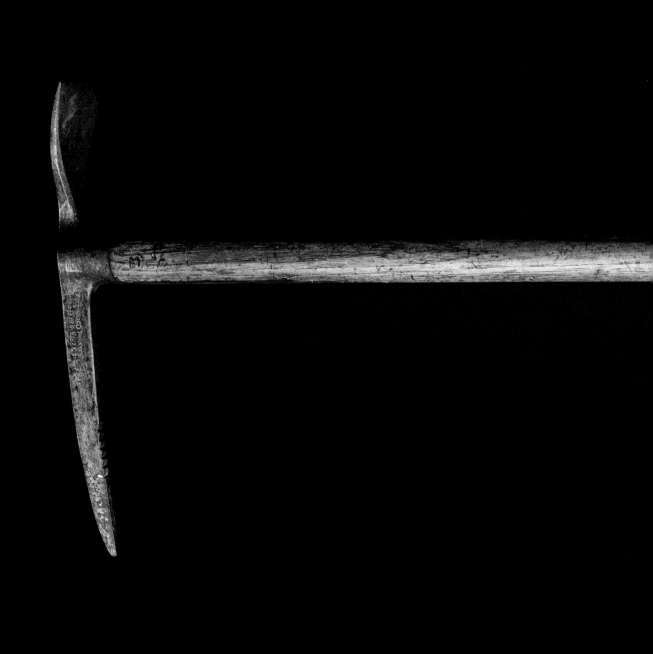

An ice axe that was used by a member
of the New Zealand party.

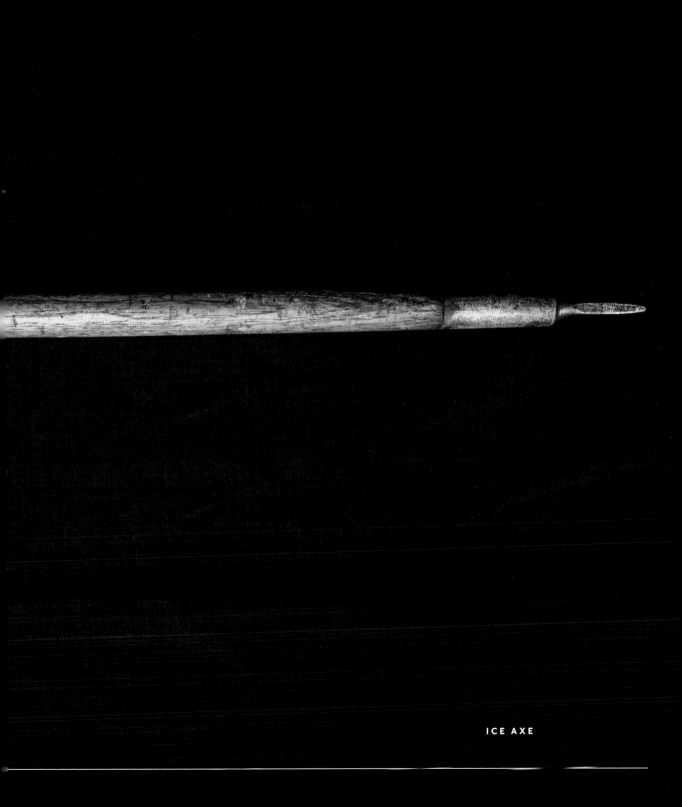

ICE AXE

On the Skelton Glacier at the same time, although in its lower reaches, were geologists Bernie Gunn and Guyon Warren, together with Arnold Heine of the summer-only IGY contingent. They carried out significant geological work in the rock cliffs and man-hauled their sledges for nearly 100 kilometres.

The proving of a route up the Skelton Glacier, rather than the Ferrar, effectively dispelled any disadvantage in siting Scott Base at Pram Point. Fortuitously, it was now the closest land-based site possible, via the Ross Ice Shelf, to the Skelton Glacier.

There remained, however, one further obstacle to overcome. Due to Marsh's illness, and the consequent abandonment of his team's journey across the Ross Ice Shelf, a route still needed to be established between Scott Base and the bottom of the Skelton Glacier. On 1 February, Miller and Roy Carlyon, a surveyor, set off across the Ross Ice Shelf with Marsh's team of eleven dogs. It was a distance of about 290 kilometres to their destination, which was estimated to take them close to two weeks. Once at the Skelton they were to survey and map its lower reaches. With the field radios having been proven to be useless, there was no direct means of communication with Scott Base but they could talk, using walkie-talkies, with a plane if it was flying overhead. This was the first time that either of these men had been in charge of a dog team and they were to learn some valuable lessons during this trip.

Sledging across the Ross Ice Shelf, although it is relatively flat, is not a simple undertaking. It is an immense body of ice, several hundred metres deep. The largest of its kind in the world, it is roughly the size of France. The surface changes from hard and polished, where the dogs slip and struggle, to soft and slushy, bringing the sledge to a crawl. Crevasses lurk, and must be picked around with care and delicacy, particularly in the regions around Black and White islands. The wind frequently hurtles along the surface, forcing men and dogs to take shelter, unable to move until it lessens.

Miller and Carlyon were making good progress despite these obstacles, but eight days into the journey trouble with the dogs began:

Tutluk the saucy little bitch in team on heat and eventually done over by Spot—caused havoc at one stage two dogs were off the trace.[30]

Even after a hard day's sledging, the dogs would not rest, and fought instead. Miller was up at 2.15 in the morning to restake the dog traces, and Carlyon up at six to do the same. 'Who made women?' a frustrated Miller recorded the next day. The following day, after setting up camp, he mentioned 'more women trouble'. In an attempt to solve this he firmly tied Tukluk to the sledge to keep her out of mischief and away from the other dogs.[31]

Through the small hours the dogs howled ceaselessly and, after a morning run, refused to start again. Eventually forcing them on, the men made only a slow couple of miles before stopping again. They had been running Tukluk at the back of the sledge, away from the pulling dogs, but clearly a different approach was required:

> As a last resort we put her on the lead trace and still the lady-in-demand took the dogs with her. An All Black pack of 10 crazed dogs surged forward never noticing the 900lbs behind them. A glorious hour of 4.6 miles absolutely knocked them. All we had to do was keep them on course.[32]

Miller and Carlyon had found the solution and there was no more trouble.

The men were ultimately successful in establishing a route from Scott Base to the bottom of the Skelton Glacier, and in carrying out significant surveying and mapping work in the lower reaches of the Skelton. On one occasion Hillary flew with Bill Cranfield in the Auster to check up on the team. Their return journey in the plane was not without its own pressures, as described in the chapter 'Bill's Flying Adventures'.

At the end of February, Miller and Carlyon were flown back to Scott Base after twenty-eight days away, the last several days of which were spent in blizzard conditions waiting at Skelton Depot for the plane to arrive to fly them back. Without means of communication with the base, they began to wonder whether they should begin the long sledging journey homeward instead. Finally, a brief weather window presented itself, and the men and dogs were flown out as quickly

Bob Miller takes a noon-sight as a way
of determining the team's location.

as possible. A tent full of equipment had to be left behind. There was no knowing, now that the autumn weather had arrived, when the plane would be able to return to pick it up.

With the return of Miller and Carlyon, and their successful reconnaissance of a route across the ice to the Skelton Glacier, the last piece of the puzzle of where to site Scott Base, and how to access the Polar Plateau, had been completed.

Miller, after his month away from the Scott Base construction site, was amazed at the progress made in his absence, and was equally pleased to see that Marsh was much better and almost back to normal:

> The Base Camp is a revelation of comfort. It's virtually completed. The covered way conveys the impression of being in a large building with many offset…we are exceptionally comfortable.[33]

Ayres was equally impressed on returning after enduring weeks of tent life during his Skelton reconnaissance trip:

> What a change to be able to walk around a hut. The chaps at Base have done magnificent work here and the establishment is a credit to their efforts. Had my first bath or wash for 6 weeks, "Super"! Drank a great deal of tea etc, a few brandies last night.[34]

With the return of the men from the Skelton Glacier, the full team of twenty-three was finally together, for the first time, in their newly built Scott Base.

**NEW ZEALAND'S FIRST WINTER-OVER
TEAM AT SCOTT BASE**

Back row, left to right: Wally Tarr, Ted Gawn, Peter MacDonald, Roy Carlyon, Murray Douglas, Richard Brooke, Bill Cranfield.

Middle row, left to right: Jim Bates, Herb Orr, Neil Sandford, Harry Ayres, Selwyn Bucknell, Guyon Warren, Peter Mulgrew, Murray Ellis.

Front row, left to right: Vern Gerard, Bernie Gunn, Ron Balham, Bob Miller, Sir Edmund Hillary, Trevor Hatherton, George Marsh, John Claydon.

LIFE AT

SCOTT BASE

FOUR

FINAL TOUCHES

As anyone who has gone through the process of having a house built or renovated can attest, there are still many things to tidy up and complete after the builders have packed up their bags and booked their offshore holiday. So it was with Scott Base.

A great flurry of activity began around constructing drawers and shelves, and partitions for the bunks. Ed had considered the question of bunks carefully in the early stages of planning the base. He was aware that Fuchs preferred all men to sleep in one bunkroom to prevent cliques being formed. Hillary, however, was of the view that each man should have his own cubicle in order to have a modicum of privacy.

Putting a twist on Ponder's original plan of one cubicle per man, Ed designed the 'Hillary

bunk'. This consisted of a normal two-tier bunk with the addition of two partitions so that the bottom bunk opened out on one side and the top bunk opened out on the other. Hatherton, rather drily, observed that the 'isolationists' of the expedition were well ahead in building these hardwood partitions even as they lagged in doing communal tasks.[1] While noting that 'the lower berths are going to provide the most spacious feeling cells',[2] he resigned himself to the fact that he didn't anticipate spending much time there 'except in the sack'.[3]

The men also laid linoleum squares, hung curtains and painted their newly built drawers. Warren, rather proudly declaring that he had chosen bright colours 'without being ghastly', installed red and black flecked curtaining with yellow and brown linoleum in his own small area. He painted grey around the bunk, his drawers blue, and finished with 'a sort of bilious greeny yellow on the outside wall and round the window'.[4] Not to be outdone, Hatherton chose a colour scheme of 'Carnation', 'Blue Haze' and 'Citron', with a blue desk and shelf tops, and declared that the whole looked 'quite attractive'.[5]

The construction of a large garage was under way by the end of February. It had a welded steel roof and was clad with the boards from empty crates. It was a huge job to take apart the crates, cart the boards to the site and then cut and nail them to fit. While helping on its construction, Warren was reminded that working in Antarctic conditions brings little challenges to otherwise everyday tasks:

> Gradually taught myself the hard way that holding nails in your mouth is not the thing to do below zero, and several little raw patches on the tongue and lips prove the truth of it.[6]

DAILY LIFE

Ed drew up a work roster so that everyone would take his turn at doing mess duties. Pairs of men were assigned for the whole week, and the jobs were many: hauling blocks of hard snow and shovelling them into the three snow-melters for water, hand-pumping the water up to each gravity tank, pumping kerosene for the generators, heaters and stoves, throwing rubbish into the pressure ridges of the sea ice, collecting cases of food from the rations dump, general cleaning, doing dishes and cooking the meals on Sundays. There was also an alphabetical bath roster; Warren noted that, as he was a 'W' he was twenty-third in a line of twenty-three, and 'so I'll go dirty for another week yet'.[7]

The various jobs were time-consuming and laborious; some, like filling the snow-melter for the kitchen, had to be done more than once a day. Inevitably, some ingenuity was employed to reduce the workload. Jim Bates, with his mechanical expertise, came up with a novel, but dubious, way of filling the huts' large kerosene tanks. Warren was impressed with its time-saving qualities and described the system in his diary:

> [We] brought back a load of kerosene and spent most of the rest of the day, between washings up, filling the hut tanks. Each hut has tanks of its own, and we now fill them by a crafty system of Jim's, whereby we blow the exhaust from a tractor in to a full drum outside, driving the kerosene through a hose into the hut tanks, instead of the laborious Ministry of Works system of hoisting full drums into each hut. Apart from the rather frightening business of watching a heavy steel drum blowing up like a balloon, and icing troubles in the hose, it works very well…[8]

The weekly work roster ended with the preparation of Sunday meals, with dinner in particular growing into an institution. Every Sunday the cook, Selwyn Bucknell, had his day off and the two expedition members who were on mess duties that week would provide the meals. It became a contest between the men as they tried to outdo each other in culinary creations. Hillary and Ayres were the first to take on this duty. They did a fine job, with game soup, curry entrée, roast beef, Yorkshire pudding, roast parsnips, boiled onion, mashed potatoes and tinned green beans, finishing with boiled pudding and custard. Ed acknowledged, on reflection, that they had made too much food and that other pairs, in time, were to show much more finesse.[9]

The meals grew to include waiting staff (usually Hatherton and Marsh) and increasingly elaborate menus that became works of art. These became canvases for various in-jokes and jibes. One menu, in beautiful Asian calligraphy, also included a thought for the week:

> From a tin to your gut,
> From your gut to a tin,
> We've done our best,
> Your tum does the rest;
> Good luck, don't bust,
> But please try to keep it in?

After three months of dinners, the fine-dining occasion on Sunday, 26 May, at the 'Southern Savoy', came with the motto: 'Se non vi piace, ess' expectorate (if you don't like it, spit it out)' together with the warning that any resemblance between the dish served and that intended would be entirely fortuitous.

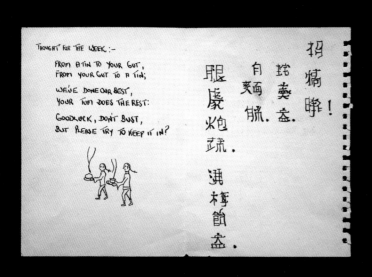

THOUGHT FOR THE WEEK :-

FROM A TIN TO YOUR GUT,
FROM YOUR GUT TO A TIN;

WE'VE DONE OUR BEST,
YOUR TUM DOES THE REST:

GOODLUCK, DON'T BUST,
BUT PLEASE TRY TO KEEP IT IN?

招痨眸！
揢羹盍.
自
麭
脓.
眼
處
炮
疏.
迅捧節盍.

PRAM-POINT HOTEL DELUX ☆☆☆☆

MENU

WITH THE COMPLIMENTS OF THE MANAGEMENT PP2-7-13

One Sunday menu with its 'thought for the week' (left)
and the cover of the 'Pram Point Hotel' menu prepared
by Bates and Mulgrew (right).

A menu prepared by Bates and Mulgrew for the 'Pram Point Hotel' included Morse code, artwork depicting Scott Base, the Beaver plane and Erebus, as well as four pages of rhyming verse parodying most of the men. Its back cover finished with the somewhat worrying line:

Two meals for the price of one
One down
One up.

With other menus proclaiming sweets as 'guaranteed fresh from the tin' and 'satisfactory meals guaranteed except on Sundays', it was clear that the men were enjoying significant entertainment during these times.

One pair, at their peril, jokingly served up pemmican for Sunday dinner. Pemmican, high in protein and fat, and designed as a staple expedition food in the polar regions, was an acquired taste — something like a combination of ground liver and peanut butter—with a rather sandy texture.[10] Bob Miller and Murray Douglas' prank backfired. Miller noted that he was 'nearly lynched',[11] Warren recorded that 'as a joke it fell rather flat',[12] and more than fifty years after the end of the expedition Peter MacDonald, an IGY technician, recalled that the men 'got the raspberry when they served a sledging meal of pemmican'.[13]

In an effort to make up for this, Miller turned to ice-cream making with gusto. By the end of March it had become a Sunday regular, but on 26 May Miller learnt a salient lesson. He put his ice cream outside the hut to set in the freezing Antarctic conditions. Just before lunch it was discovered that it had all but disappeared. Through the dim light of the polar night, Miller made out the telltale signs of the culprits—many sets of footprints from excited husky pups that had sensed an opportunity and helped themselves. Some of the men reported lapping noises coming from the darkness as the puppies ate their way through it.[14] 'Miller was *not* pleased.'[15]

IDES OF MARCH

An artwork from Bob Miller's collection
of memorabilia from winter 1957.

LAST OUTINGS BEFORE WINTER

Many of the men managed to squeeze in some brief sledging journeys before winter set in. Ed, Mulgrew, Ellis and Bates set off on a test trip in the tractors to Cape Crozier in mid-March,[16] and in early April, Brooke and Gunn took dogs and travelled 40 kilometres across the Ross Ice Shelf to White Island to carry out glaciological studies.

The last field trip was in late April, when many of the men travelled by foot or dog team, following the coast of Ross Island, to Cape Evans where Captain Scott's famous final expedition hut sits. The journey, although relatively short, was a challenge with its mixture of sea-ice travel, steep climbs, equally steep descents and errant dogs. An offshore wind grew in strength, threatening to blow the sea ice out into the vast Ross Sea and the

men with it. They climbed up and over the very steep Erebus Glacier ice tongue, a massive protrusion streaming down from the volcano to McMurdo Sound. Marsh's sledge brake disintegrated on the vertiginous descent and, horrified that his charging dogs were going to plunge into a crevasse at the bottom, he overturned his sledge to force a stop. Meanwhile, as Ayres was helping Marsh get his team sorted again, his own dogs took off. Gunn managed to throw himself on to the empty sledge as it hurtled past but it still took him over a mile on the sea ice to stop them.[17]

Captain Scott's hut had been built in 1911, the year he arrived in McMurdo Sound on *Terra Nova*. The sea ice was so thick on that occasion that he had to be content with Cape

The radio room was the
domain of one of Hillary's closest
allies and most loyal friends, Peter
Mulgrew, as well as radio operator
Ted Gawn. Radio equipment consisted
of older World War II Morse and
HF transmitters.

PREVIOUS PAGE AND ABOVE: Equipment
in the radio room in Hut A (Hillary's hut).

Evans for a base rather than pushing on further south to his earlier expedition hut at Hut Point (where the American base now sits). By 1957 Captain Scott's hut was in a sadly decrepit state after over forty years of absence and neglect:

> By climbing over the roof of the lean-to 'stables' you can get into the main messroom through a window — this room is ice free but everything else is entirely choked.
> A completely indescribable shambles inside — the table and floor and even rafters littered with tins and bottles, tools, penguin eggs, rope, an old bicycle sprocket and pedal, and all covered in black grime from the iron stove. A colossal amount of food of all kinds piled up in boxes and on all the shelves around, and bales of straw, the remains of the old motor sledge and lots of ironmongery outside.[18]

WINTER

Settling down for the long, dark winter the men, when not on mess duties, still had plenty of work to do. Hillary, Bates and Ellis were busy in the garage modifying the three tractors and sledges, and building a caboose, for the attempt to drive up to the Polar Plateau the following spring. The IGY team, with International Geophysical Year officially beginning on 1 July, was busy with their equipment, observations and experiments. Scientific work included ionospheric investigation, earthquake recording, testing of radio propagation, recording of solar radiation, tidal movements, 24-hour observations of the aurora australis and, in a special hut constructed of non-magnetic materials, continuous recording of the earth's magnetic field.[19]

The dogs took a lot of looking after. They needed to be shifted on to fresh ice, exercised and fed. The men had killed dozens of seals over the summer and autumn and these frozen carcasses had to be painstakingly sawed into chunks manageable for the dogs to chew. Even back in February when there were only twenty-nine dogs to care for, the rest being out in the field, it was a long business, and it took all afternoon to feed them.[20] Ayres recalled that, during a particularly vicious mid-June storm, the dog lines became covered in layers of snow. If it had kept up, the dogs would have had to be turned loose. Once buried beneath the snowdrift, and trapped by their lines, there was a real risk of a number of the dogs dying from suffocation. The frozen seals were inaccessible, as they were under four feet of snow, and the hungry dogs had been tossed some canned meat, which was 'not so good'.[21]

Of the nine buildings at Scott Base, the heart of base life was centred around the first of those constructed, Hut A. Just 12 metres by 6 metres (39 feet x 20 feet), it comprised four main spaces — the mess room, Hillary's office, the radio room and the kitchen.

The mess room was the focal point of base life for the wintering party of twenty-three — the eighteen TAE members and the five IGY members. In addition to being the place where they ate meals it also doubled as the library, chapel, briefing room and heart of social activities. A bright blue Shacklock 501 range provided warmth. On the wall hung framed pictures of the TAE patron, Queen Elizabeth II, and the Duke of Edinburgh, who had entertained the men aboard HMY *Britannia* in Lyttelton Harbour before they departed for McMurdo Sound.

The kitchen was sizeable and included a large snow-melter, ensuring a continuous supply of fresh water. Beside it stood the large No. 2 President cooker, the realm of Selwyn Bucknell as he fed the expedition members. It was here that the men toiled away on Sundays when on mess duty.

The radio room was the link to home. As there were no ships or aircraft able to operate during the winter months, the men could neither receive nor send mail. In an age without internet or satellite communication their only means of communication with their loved ones back home was through radio. The radio room was the domain of one of Hillary's closest allies and most loyal friends, Peter Mulgrew, as well as radio operator Ted Gawn. Radio equipment consisted of older World War II Morse and HF transmitters.

Given the high cost of transmission there was a strict allotment of calls home to loved ones. Many of the members had young families and the weekly call home was a special occasion, greatly looked forward to. The men, however, were often left disappointed and uneasy. There was so much

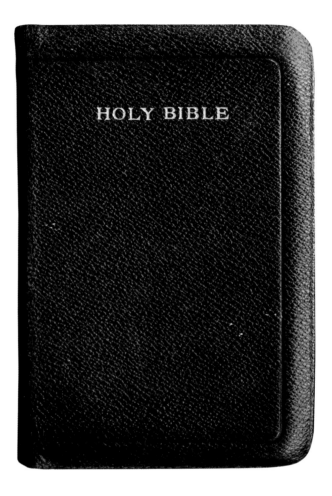

BOB MILLER'S BIBLE

to talk about, but the calls were regularly affected by atmospherics and full of noisy static and delays. The position of chief radio operator, though, had its perks, with Mulgrew's wife recalling getting two, not one, calls a week from Antarctica.[22]

Hillary's office was directly off the mess room. On Ponder's original plan it was intended to house Hillary's desk and filing cabinet. But with the late addition of Douglas to the wintering-over party, occupying the bunk Hillary had intended for himself in Hut C, a change of plan was needed. Ed instead constructed his bed along

the wall in Hut A that was intended to house the filing cabinet. Unfortunately, trying to get to sleep so close to the hub of base life would, on occasion, lead to grumbles, particularly from some of the men who wished to socialise late into the night.

The final section of the hut was a cold porch which led to the covered corrugated-iron passageway. The ability to walk between the majority of the buildings without having to go outside was greatly envied by their American neighbours.

3 I am weary of my crying: my throat is dried: mine eyes fail while I wait for my God.

4 They that hate me without a cause are more than the hairs of mine head: they that would destroy me, being mine enemies wrongfully, are mighty: then I restored that which I took not away.

5 O God, thou knowest my foolishness; and my sins are not hid from thee.

6 Let not them that wait on thee, O Lord God of hosts, be ashamed for my sake; let not those that seek thee be confounded for my sake, O God of Israel.

7 Because for thy sake I have borne reproach; shame hath covered my face.

8 I am become a stranger unto my brethren, and an alien unto my mother's children.

9 For the zeal of thine house hath eaten me up; and the reproaches of them that reproached thee are fallen upon me.

10 When I wept, and chastened my soul with fasting, that was to my reproach.

11 I made sackcloth also my garment; and I became a proverb to them.

12 They that sit in the gate speak against me; and I was the song of the drunkards.

13 But as for me, my prayer is unto thee, O Lord, in an acceptable time: O God, in the multitude of thy mercy hear me, in the truth of thy salvation.

14 Deliver me out of the mire, and let me not sink: let me be delivered from them that hate me, and out of the deep waters.

15 Let not the waterflood overflow me, neither let the deep swallow me up, and let not the pit shut her mouth upon me.

16 Hear me, O Lord; for thy lovingkindness is good: turn unto me according to the multitude of thy tender mercies.

17 And hide not thy face from thy servant; for I am in trouble: hear me speedily.

18 Draw nigh unto my soul, and redeem it: deliver me because of mine enemies.

19 Thou hast known my reproach, and my shame, and my dishonour: mine adversaries are all before thee.

20 Reproach hath broken my heart; and I am full of heaviness: and I looked for some to take pity, but there was none; and for comforters, but I found none.

21 They gave me also gall for my meat; and in my thirst they gave me vinegar to drink.

22 Let their table become a snare before them: and that which should have been for their welfare, let it become a trap.

23 Let their eyes be darkened, that they see not; and make their loins continually to shake.

24 Pour out thine indignation upon them, and let thy wrathful anger take hold of them.

25 Let their habitation be desolate; and let none dwell in their tents.

26 For they persecute him whom thou hast smitten; and they talk to the grief of those whom thou hast wounded.

27 Add iniquity unto their iniquity: and let them not come into thy righteousness.

28 Let them be blotted out of the book of the living, and not be written with the righteous.

29 But I am poor and sorrowful: let thy salvation, O God, set me up on high.

30 I will praise the name of God with a song, and will magnify him with thanksgiving.

31 This also shall please the Lord better than an ox or bullock that hath horns and hoofs.

32 The humble shall see this, and be glad: and your heart shall live that seek God.

33 For the Lord heareth the poor, and despiseth not his prisoners.

34 Let the heaven and earth praise him, the seas, and every thing that moveth therein.

35 For God will save Zion, and will build the cities of Judah: that they may dwell there, and have it in possession.

36 The seed also of his servants shall inherit it: and they that love his name shall dwell therein.

PSALM 70

To the chief Musician, A Psalm of David, to bring to remembrance.

MAKE haste, O God, to deliver me; make haste to help me, O Lord.

2 Let them be ashamed and confounded that seek after my soul: let them be turned backward, and put to confusion, that desire my hurt.

3 Let them be turned back for a reward of their shame that say, Aha, Aha.

4 Let all those that seek thee rejoice and be glad in thee: and let such as love thy salvation say continually, Let God be magnified.

5 But I am poor and needy: make haste unto me, O God: thou art my help and my deliverer; O Lord, make no tarrying.

PSALM 71

IN thee, O Lord, do I put my trust: let me never be put to confusion.

2 Deliver me in thy righteousness, and cause me to escape: incline thine ear unto me, and save me.

3 Be thou my strong habitation, whereunto I may continually resort: thou hast given commandment to save me; for thou art my rock and my fortress.

4 Deliver me, O my God, out of the hand of the wicked, out of the hand of the unrighteous and cruel man.

5 For thou art my hope, O Lord God: thou art my trust from my youth.

6 By thee have I been holden up from the womb: thou art he that took me out of my mother's bowels: my praise shall be continually of thee.

7 I am as a wonder unto many; but thou art my strong refuge.

8 Let my mouth be filled with thy praise and with thy honour all the day.

9 Cast me not off in the time of old age; forsake me not when my strength faileth.

10 For mine enemies speak against me; and they that lay wait for my soul take counsel together,

11 Saying, God hath forsaken him: persecute and take him; for there is none to deliver him.

12 O God, be not far from me: O my God, make haste for my help.

13 Let them be confounded and consumed that are adversaries to my soul; let them be covered with reproach and dishonour that seek my hurt.

14 But I will hope continually, and will yet praise thee more and more.

15 My mouth shall shew forth thy righteousness and thy salvation all the day; for I know not the numbers thereof.

16 I will go in the strength of the Lord God: I will make mention of thy righteousness, even of thine only.

17 O God, thou hast taught me from my youth: and hitherto have I declared thy wondrous works.

18 Now also when I am old and greyheaded, O God, forsake me not; until I have shewed thy strength unto this generation, and thy power to every one that is to come.

19 Thy righteousness also, O God, is very high, who hast done great things: O God, who is like unto thee!

20 Thou, which hast shewed me great and sore troubles, shalt quicken me again, and shalt bring me up again from the depths of the earth.

21 Thou shalt increase my greatness, and comfort me on every side.

22 I will also praise thee with the psaltery, even thy truth, O my God: unto thee will I sing with the harp, O thou Holy One of Israel.

23 My lips shall greatly rejoice when I sing unto thee; and my soul, which thou hast redeemed.

24 My tongue also shall talk of thy righteousness all the day long: for they are confounded, for they are brought unto shame, that seek my hurt.

PSALM 72

A Psalm for Solomon.

GIVE the king thy judgments, O God, and thy righteousness unto the king's son.

2 He shall judge thy people with righteousness, and thy poor with judgment.

3 The mountains shall bring peace to the people, and the little hills, by righteousness.

4 He shall judge the poor of the people, he shall save the children of the needy, and shall break in pieces the oppressor.

5 They shall fear thee as long as the sun and moon endure, throughout all generations.

For entertainment, there were many books, board games, table tennis, soccer and trips to the Americans at Hut Point. Long, competitive games of bridge, often including the Americans, were a favourite activity with many of the men. Ludo became popular and, with a record player and about 500 vinyl records, there was much music to choose from. Two songs were particular favourites with at least some of the men: Doris Day's 'The Black Hills of Dakota' and Julie Andrews' 'Getting to Know You'. Ed became so sick of hearing the latter that he broke the record.[23]

Saturday nights, changing to Sunday nights by midwinter, became party nights with much good cheer. By April, the half-hour or so before Saturday dinner had become rather like a cocktail party. The men did their best to socialise as they would, no doubt, have done back in their home environments. But there was no escaping the obvious lack of female company:

> Most people tidy up a bit, someone brews a cocktail or punch and keeps the glasses filled, and everyone stands around nattering. It gets pretty crowded and smoky which adds to the resemblance, but there's one sad lack which can't ever be remedied down here.[24]

There was plenty of alcohol available for those who wanted it, with 'beer and rum unlimited, 24 hrs a day, whiskey, brandy, gin etc etc on Saturday nights and any special occasions, a bottle (small) of wine apiece on Sundays, to deaden the shock of the amateur cooking'.[25] Dominion Breweries supplied the beer, although apparently not as much as requested, and many of the beer bottles were cracked before they could be got into the warmth of the hut.[26] The government-issued navy rum was not, according to Cranfield, to everyone's liking. The men were not above making a few homegrown cocktails and a concoction was soon devised which also helped to reduce the ample stocks of condensed milk. The result, 'moose's milk', was made up of equal parts of rum, boiling water and condensed milk, mixed in a beer glass. For those wanting to ward off scurvy, a dash of rosehip syrup was optional.[27]

With the true onset of the endless darkness of winter, and the initial excitement of life in Antarctica waning, each of the twenty-three men must have faced challenges living and working in such close confinement. Some of the men either struggled to keep writing in their diaries or stopped altogether, work programmes became tedious, some temperaments were irascible and there were occasional angry outbursts. Hatherton expressed his frustration in his diary, writing in May 1957 'that we should be getting much more [scientific] work done', and in June, 'there is a great tendency at present to criticise others. Not free from it myself but must purge it out of my system.'[28] Ayres wrote that, by June, 'most of the chaps have been just doing odd work which is necessary otherwise taking things easy' and that 'only 4 or 6 chaps rise before lunch on Sundays'.[29]

A divine service was held at midday on Sundays, including readings and singing, and the first service was fairly well attended. Perhaps due to the general slowing down of activities in the heart of winter, however, by mid-June the numbers had dwindled to four.[30]

Some of the men were also becoming frustrated at the lack of certainty over the spring and summer sledging journeys. Ed was busy trying to manage the ambit of the New Zealand party's responsibilities towards the TAE, the wishes of the geologists and surveyors to explore and document new, or sparsely understood, territory, and his own ambition to drive tractors up to the Polar Plateau and beyond. The latter plan, in particular, did not have much popular support among the men, with the 'anti-tractorites' comprising 'almost the whole works except Ed'.[31] Ed was, however, determined: 'irrespective of the opinions of others I knew what I wanted to do and was determined to push it through—despite secret doubts at times as to its feasibility'.[32] The competing demands for men, dogs, fuel, equipment and air support led to plans, amended plans and yet more plans. Tension and uncertainty grew.

The men looked for occasions for celebration or entertainment, and on 29 May Miller produced a cake shaped and iced like Everest, to mark the fourth anniversary of Ed's achievement. Ayres, who had originally been selected for the 1953 Everest expedition, made a speech in Hillary's honour,[33] and noted, 'Old Ed was surprised and I'm sure quite pleased to think we had remembered.'[34]

PREVIOUS PAGE AND BELOW:
The mess room in Hut A (Hillary's hut).

PAGE 80: Features of the mess room, including the Shacklock 501 range on the south wall (top left) and the extractor fan on the west wall (top right).

PREVIOUS PAGE: Marcus King's oil painting 'High Country Muster' adorns the north wall of the mess room.

THIS PAGE: Portraits of the Duke of Edinburgh and Queen Elizabeth II in the mess room (left) and the telephone with directory underneath (right).

FACING PAGE: The original Vigilant fire alarm box in the mess room (right).

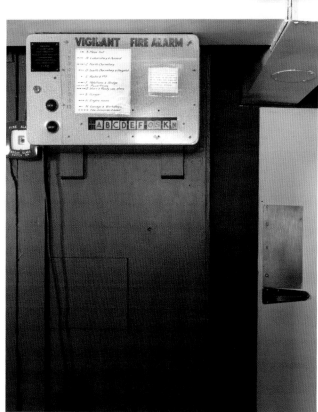

With the true onset of the endless darkness of winter, and the initial excitement of life in Antarctica waning, each of the twenty-three men must have faced challenges living and working in such close confinement.

Ed Hillary shares a laugh with some
of the other men at Scott Base.

In the tradition of the expeditions of the 'heroic era' of the early twentieth century, midwinter was a milestone that could not go uncelebrated. The men held a festive dinner on 21 June, with all the trimmings:

> Cocktails at six—everyone in a clean shirt, and some pretence at creases in the trousers, and several even with ties … Richard arrived complete with cocktail frock (tent inner), lipstick, spray, ankle socks and smart sunhat, on George's arm; and at the other extreme, Bernie rather ridiculous in a suit. Each place with a personal menu—a portrait of the owner by Bill, and beautifully lettered inside by Bob. A colossal amount of work in it. Meal started at seven, served by George and Trevor in white jackets, and a very fine feast at that. All the usual doings plus champagne—some of this massaged by George into Ron's bald patch to stimulate the growth. A long series of toasts, fortunately none of them too serious as there were inclined to be occasional interjections.[35]

The party continued raucously until finally Ed quietened the men down. Keen to continue partying, a group drifted off to the sledge room. Ayres eventually went to bed at 2 am, to be 'rudely awakened by George [Marsh], Peter [Mulgrew] and Bob [Miller] who insisted upon singing to me. They then did the rounds and kept people awake 'till 6 am.'[36]

During winter, Ed also instigated a weekly lecture series with an eclectic collection of (mostly) light-hearted subjects, with each man taking his turn at presenting.[37] These talks, held on Tuesdays at 4 pm, were generally well received and attended (see sample schedule opposite).

7 MAY

CROCODILE HUNTING IN THE SOLOMON ISLANDS

by Ed Hillary

|

14 MAY

BULL-FIGHTING — BLOOD AND TEQUILA IN MEXICO CITY

by Don Roberto Miller

|

21 MAY

WALLABY AND OPOSSUM CONTROL IN NEW ZEALAND

by the man who dun it — Sel Bucknell

|

28 MAY

WHY AN AEROPLANE FLIES

by Bill Cranfield (This has nothing to do with bus driving)

|

4 JUN

INTERPLANETARY TRAVEL

by Vern Gerard (The usual IGY science-fiction)

|

11 JUN

GLACIOLOGY

by Bernie Gunn (A reasoned discourse on why ice is slippery)

|

18 JUN

TRAPPING IN NORTH-EAST GREENLAND

by Richard Brooke (About as fur as he went)

25 JUN

THE ART OF SACKING

by Murray Ellis (Why you should buy an Ellis sleeping bag)

|

2 JUL

MODERN DEVELOPMENTS IN RADIO

by Ted Gawn (Some information on the crystal set)

|

9 JUL

IS THE IGY PARTY AT SCOTT BASE REALLY NECESSARY?

by Dr Hatherton (This is a rhetorical question. Any resemblance to fact will be purely coincidental)

|

16 JUL

GAS-TURBINE ENGINES AS RELATED TO AIRCRAFT PROPULSION

by Wally Tarr (Apparently the pilot isn't the only thing that keeps a plane flying)

|

23 JUL

CLIMBING IN THE SOUTHERN ALPS

by Harry Ayres (The thrilling story of the man who accompanied Sir Edmund Hillary on some of his great climbs)

|

30 JUL

PAINTING

by Peter MacDonald (To hell with photographic reproduction!)

|

6 AUG

APPROACH TO ASTRONOMY

by James Jeans Bates (How you can build a hundred-inch telescope!)

13 AUG

SPENDING £150,000

by Roy Carlyon (Why we pay so much in taxes)

|

20 AUG

IDYLLS IN THE BANANA BELT

by Dr George Marsh (Sweating through the jungle at Hope Bay — the FIDS base in Grahamland)

|

27 AUG

FISHING

by John Claydon (Tall tails and long arms)

|

3 SEPT

THIN SECTIONING

by Guy Warren (Probably about hardboard)

|

10 SEPT

EARTHQUAKES I HAVE KNOWN

by Peter Mulgrew (There will only be a brief mention of Ellis)

|

17 SEPT

HUDSON BAY

by Dr Ron Balham (An illustrated lecture in glorious kodachrome. Unfortunately Ron has forgotten to bring his slides)

|

24 SEPT

THE IONOSPHERE

by Neil Sandford (An explanation of QRM and the Heterodyne Hum)

|

1 OCT

THE TECHNIQUE OF MOUNTAINEERING

by Murray Douglas (How to negotiate the difficult pitch between the Hermitage Bar and Unwin Hut)

They battled winds so ferocious that the dog teams were blown off their feet. The men were forced to dig a separate hole in the ice for each dog to shelter in, as they could not maintain a grip on the ice.

More serious lectures and lessons were also held, with an eye to the forthcoming summer expeditions. After the failure of the field radio sets the previous summer, resulting in the mercy dash to raise the alarm for the ailing Marsh, new sets had been ordered. These could only, however, transmit in Morse code. Throughout winter Gawn gave Morse lessons to the field parties and the pilots. Classes were also held, instructed by Miller, in polar navigation. As the men who travelled up and on to the Plateau the following summer were to learn, poor navigation led to inconvenience and, at the very least, greatly increased the overall risk of polar travel.

SPRING

On 23 August the sun made a tentative return. From then on, daylight grew in length and strength until, on 9 September, the first of the spring journeys began.

Marsh and Warren travelled north of Captain Scott's hut at Cape Evans and inspected the smaller, more homely base at Cape Royds, which had been established by Shackleton during his 1907–09 expedition. Warren found it to be 'much more sanitary and altogether more pleasant than Evans. Door and passage almost blocked with snow but burrowed in. Very clean inside and relatively tidy.'[38] They then travelled west, across the frozen McMurdo Sound, to the Ferrar Glacier where by arrangement they met Miller and Carlyon, inspected the Ferrar and concluded that it remained too rough to negotiate. Brooke and Gunn also crossed McMurdo Sound for surveying and geologising work in the Blue Glacier area. Hillary, accompanied by Bates, Ellis, Mulgrew and Herb Orr, took three tractors and left food and fuel depots at Butter Point and Gneiss Point for use by sledging parties later in the season.

Ayres, Douglas, Dr Ron Balham and Neil Sandford, forcing their way to the emperor penguin rookery at Cape Crozier, battled winds so ferocious that the dog teams were blown off their feet. The men were forced to dig a separate hole in the ice for each dog to shelter in, as they could not maintain a grip on the ice. Some other trips of short duration also took place as the men readied themselves and their dogs for the summer ahead.

Plans were still evolving for the summer, and the frequent changes and uncertainty were causing frustrations for some of the team. After being cooped up all winter the men were keen to get out and explore. The last Sunday dinner with all twenty-three men of the New Zealand party was held on 29 September, and in a light-hearted dig at their leader a reminder of the expedition's plan changes was produced:

> a very good speech from John [Claydon], presenting Ed a pictorial Plan X (we've had and discarded Plans A to W already) painted by Bill [Cranfield].[39]

By early October the first of the summer sledging parties, the Northern Party,[40] had departed. Ten days later, Ed and his team departed on the tractors for their attempt to drive up to the vast Polar Plateau. Dog teams and their drivers followed shortly after. Scott Base had performed beautifully over the winter but it was now time to move on to the next stage of the New Zealand adventure.

Guyon Warren and Murray Douglas preparing to leave Scott Base in a survey party.

Sir Edmund Hillary, Derek Wright and Murray Ellis
on the Ferguson tractors at the South Pole.

THE
TRACTOR
JOURNEY

FIVE

It was hardly a great start. Despite giving Ed's team a warm send-off on 14 October 1957, the men of Scott Base and the Americans from Hut Point were exceedingly doubtful. It was a commonly held, and not secret, opinion that the three tractors would founder somewhere on the Ross Ice Shelf. As expedition objectives go, it was audacious.

Attempting to drive three Ferguson tractors, and a Weasel, nearly 300 kilometres along the route that Miller, Carlyon and their dogs had reconnoitred the autumn before would be difficult enough. They were then to ascend the 145-kilometre length of the Skelton Glacier, with its maze of crevasses, its katabatic winds and the forbiddingly steep 'steps' up to its full height of 2400 metres, and then on to the cold and seemingly endless

Polar Plateau. Providing support for Fuchs' TAE crossing party meant that, once on the Plateau, they would need to drive for hundreds of miles, setting up depots as they went. In the seemingly unlikely event that the tractors succeeded in completing that task, Ed intended to go even further.

It would have been difficult for the four drivers—Hillary, Ellis, Mulgrew and Balham—to argue against such pessimism. Although dog teams had travelled this way, tractors are not dogs. They have myriad mechanical moving parts, which are prone to wearing and breaking in the cold, fuel that goes sluggish and freezes, a clumsy heaviness that makes them the 'perfect crevasse detectors',[1] and a fatal disposition towards rolling should the terrain prove too steep. And should they die, or if there is an emergency, you can't eat them.

Four and a half hours after starting, the men had managed to travel only 10.5 kilometres from Scott Base. They were towing 11 tonnes of supplies on sledges that had to be forced over pressure ridges formed by the immense forces between sea ice and ice shelf. The surface of the Ross Ice Shelf varied from hard and crusty through to soft and sticky. The tractors disliked softness and churned slowly and wearily through it, sinking into the soft snow. Crevasses lay hidden in areas that the men thought would be free of them, and within the first few hours one of the sledges had tipped half over into a crevasse. It had to be unloaded of its cumbersome 150-kilogram drums before being righted, reattached to a tractor and reloaded.

The men must have been hoping, as they wearily set up camp later that evening, that they could not be seen from Scott Base and that no aerial reconnaissance would be carried out to establish their position. The early lack of progress would be embarrassing, especially considering the enormous hurdles that lay ahead.

Seven months earlier the vehicles had undergone their first real test in preparation for the journey. On 19 March the same team, with the exception of Bates in place of Balham, had set off to travel to Cape Crozier. This is a notoriously windswept promontory on Ross Island, made famous by three members of Scott's last expedition, Henry Bowers, Bill Wilson and Apsley Cherry-Garrard. Their story was immortalised in Cherry-Garrard's memoir *The Worst Journey in the World*, which described the breathtakingly horrendous deprivations and conditions that they suffered as they man-hauled their sledges through the dark Antarctic winter in search of an emperor penguin colony at the Cape.

For Ed and his team, however, the conditions were different. It was autumn not winter, and although they endured freezing conditions and biting winds, it was no comparison to the pitch-black hell that Bowers' team experienced. And, of course, the New Zealanders were travelling in two large vehicles. The purpose of the trip was not to compare steadfastness—although Ed did take a copy of Cherry-Garrard's book—but to test the 'roadworthiness' of the Ferguson tractors. They

An artwork from Bob Miller's collection of memorabilia from winter 1957.

CTOR RATIONS FOR TRACTOR DRIVERS

The March journey to Cape Crozier led the men to make a number of modifications to the tractors...In the large garage at Scott Base, Ellis and Bates completely overhauled the vehicles.

FACING PAGE: This Ferguson TE-20 tractor, used by Hillary's tractor party to reach the South Pole, is on display at Canterbury Museum.

FOLLOWING PAGES: The grill (left) and track (right) on the Ferguson TE-20 tractor that now resides at Canterbury Museum.

were each towing 1.5 tonnes of supplies, and the conditions were at times extremely difficult. The tractors laboured in soft snow, the men were nervous and alert to hidden crevasses, and the final leg of the outward route up on to the Cape was steep and precipitous. Using Cherry-Garrard's account as a reference, the men searched for the shelter that the earlier explorers had made. They were delighted to find it, together with a large number of artefacts, which they carefully listed and returned for safekeeping.

Taking just twelve hours to cover the distance that had taken the famed 1911 explorers weeks, the New Zealanders learned a great deal about the capacity of the tractors to cope in the icy conditions, and their own abilities to improvise. On the trip home, finding that the fuel in one of the tractors kept freezing, Bates and Mulgrew took extreme action. Lighting blowtorches, they carefully heated the fuel tank and fuel line just enough to get things back in a liquid state and the tractor moving again. Hillary and Ellis, perhaps showing a sensible lack of solidarity in view of the risk of explosion, stood well back!

The March journey to Cape Crozier led the men to make a number of modifications to the tractors in preparation for the journey they were to undertake seven months later. In the large garage at Scott Base, Ellis and Bates completely overhauled the vehicles and Hillary, having found the experience of sitting on the sledge, when taking a rest from driving, impossibly cold and uncomfortable, constructed a 'caboose'. This looked like a horsebox on skis, and was designed to be towed behind the tractors or the Weasel. He fitted it out with bunks, cupboards, a cooking bench with primus stoves, and radio equipment.

At least one of Hillary's Scott Base team scathingly wondered about the caboose's ability to withstand the first good wind it encountered.[2] Regardless, Hillary was, without doubt, rather pleased and quietly proud of his creation, perhaps because carpentry was not his greatest skill. After assessing his attempts at furniture-making for his bunk-bed space at Scott Base, his team had, tongue in cheek, awarded him with a 'Woodsman 2nd Class' badge.[3]

Members of the tractor party, from left to right:
Sir Edmund Hillary, Murray Ellis, Jim Bates
and Peter Mulgrew.

In October 1957, and with the caboose's first night out on the Ross Ice Shelf now over, Hillary, Ellis, Mulgrew and Balham woke in good spirits and with a steady determination to put some real distance between themselves and Scott Base. Their first destination was Skelton Depot, a cache of food and fuel that had been stored at the base of the Skelton Glacier during the preceding summer. Despite the continuing soft snow conditions the men nearly quadrupled their distance of the day before, which was just as well, because the following morning a US naval plane swooped low over them and landed on the snow. Out popped a New Zealand Cabinet minister and the American ambassador to New Zealand, as well as press reporters and cameramen. The VIPs wished the men well before reboarding their plane and roaring back to McMurdo Sound, taking only a few minutes to cover the distance that had taken the land vehicles two long days.

It was five days before the men made it to their first destination. Waiting for them at Skelton Depot were three of their colleagues, and two teams of dogs, who had been deposited by plane. Bates, suffering from the effects of the flu, was to join the tractor journey. Miller and Marsh were to scale the Skelton Glacier using dog teams, travelling in unison with the tractors for the mutual benefit and safety of both expeditions. If they made it to the top of the Skelton Glacier, all the men would be

needed to help with the stocking, with air support, of the Plateau Depot.

The men, however, were forced to remain at Skelton Depot for the next three days. The Weasel had suffered severe mechanical problems during the crossing of the ice shelf and its engine had to be lifted out in order to replace the problem part. Using two huge lengths of timber, brought along in case of a crevasse rescue, Bates and Miller set up a bipod and suspended a block and tackle from it. A hole was cut in the roof of the Weasel, through which a rope was threaded and, with no doubt some considerable manoeuvring, the engine was lifted out.

The Weasel, unlike the three Fergusons, was a dedicated snow vehicle with excellent traction in soft snow conditions. It could operate on steep, soft terrain, pulling loads in a manner that the tractors could not. Hillary had observed its characteristics the summer before when he travelled to the Weddell Sea with Fuchs to establish Shackleton Base. Unfortunately for the New Zealand party, Weasels came with hefty price tags. The Ross Sea Committee turned to Ferguson tractors instead and the Weasel that now formed part of Ed's team was on loan from the Americans courtesy of the generosity of Rear Admiral Dufek.

One of the Ferguson tractors, with the
Weasel and caboose alongside.

The tractors, Weasel and dog teams began the ascent of the Skelton Glacier on 22 October. The glacier is approximately 145 kilometres long, rising to a height of over 2400 metres above the Ross Ice Shelf.[4] For Marsh and Miller, driving their dogs, the first few days were horrendous. The surface was slick and hard. The men struggled to keep their feet and, hurtling along behind their excited dog teams, they each capsized their sledges several times on the first day—Miller seven times and Marsh six. They tried to help each other set the sledges upright but sometimes they capsized at the same time, some distance apart, and then there was no alternative but for each man to unload his entire sledge, haul it upright and then reload:

> Early in the day I was almost one mile ahead of Geo[rge] and thinking he was a long way behind I looked through the binoculars to find him over and unloading. I turned my boys round and began to race back full of justification and a little satisfaction that I was able to help Geo who had just helped me right my sledge. Two chaps with a real heave can put a sledge on its runners again but one must unload completely. So I ran back and capsized after 50 yards. So there was Geo and I both unloading sledges a mile apart—the air was electric at my end and Geo later said it was thunderous around him. On our later many capsizes we took it more philosophically and laughed it off.[5]

Two days later the men encountered more difficulties, but from a different quarter. Katabatic winds, which drain from a place of high elevation down a slope, are notoriously fierce in Antarctica. The winds that funnel along the huge glaciers, running from the Polar Plateau down to sea level, can reach hurricane speeds, scouring the ice and hurling debris. Into this, the men drove their dogs until it was impossible to go or see any further. They managed just over 3 kilometres on the second day of their ascent and were forced to shelter behind the only barrier available, their sledges. Into this maelstrom, having set out after the dogs, the tractors roared past, less than 20 metres away. The drivers in their cabs were oblivious, in the murk and noise, to the huddling men and dogs. Marsh and Miller, expecting the

vehicles to stop, watched helplessly as they went on by.

The two men dared not run over to alert the tractors. To do this, leaving the relative shelter of the sledges, would be to risk becoming disorientated in the blizzard and unable to find their way back to safety. With huge difficulty they set up a tent in which to wait out the storm. Miller had become ill with the same flu that had afflicted Bates, and as soon as he could he crawled into his sleeping bag and fell asleep. His coughing was so bad that Marsh made a special trip out into the blizzard to their stores to retrieve some aspirin and brandy for him. It is difficult to imagine a more uncomfortable sickbed.

Meanwhile, the tractors made fairly good progress on the shiny, hard surface. The men were able to keep driving into the onslaught for a full 29 kilometres. While Miller and Marsh, with their dogs, were confined to their toehold on the glacier, the tractors continued grinding forward and upwards each day. The wind rarely gave them a reprieve. Layers of wind-blown snow would often hide the yawning openings of hidden crevasses of immense depth. The layers of snow can build up and up to form relatively sturdy bridges across which dogs and their sledges can cross safely, but not the weight of a vehicle. To sense the presence of crevasses in the poor visibility was a challenge.

The first crevasses they struck were relatively small and some of the snow bridges held. As they pushed on, however, the snow bridges would collapse. The vehicles inevitably lurched violently as the ground disappeared beneath their back tracks, the momentum of their forward motion driving them out of danger. This worked relatively well as long as the crevasses remained narrow. They crossed, by their calculations, about a hundred crevasses in this way. Hillary took the view that this was 'no place for too much caution or crossing the area would have taken us days',[6] admitting, however, the unpleasantness of looking back and seeing gaping holes where moments before there had been solid snow.

Larger crevasses, which had been spied by the pilots' aerial reconnaissance in preparation for the journey, nestled beneath a massive rock feature that the men called 'Clinker Bluff'. This area was strictly avoided, forcing them to take a route up steadily steepening snow slopes—'the Staircases'. This would be where the true test of the tractors lay. Their forte was most definitely not in steep slopes, particularly if the snow conditions were soft. Grinding their way upward, the tractors got further than expected but eventually could go no more. Sledges were unhitched and the vehicles, working in unison to haul the loads, painstakingly crawled higher before unhitching the sledges and driving back down to collect the ones left behind. Relaying in this fashion was slow and arduous but it worked. They crawled ever higher until forced into a narrow gully with great crevasses lining the route. Carefully guiding the vehicles, with frightening holes lying short metres away on either side, they squeezed their way to the steepest slope yet.

Hillary knew that the steep slope rising up before them would be the toughest for the tractors. If they failed at this point, there was no other route up the glacier. This would not spell the end of the depot laying for the TAE, for the dog teams and air transport would continue the work. Hillary, however, well aware of the general lack of confidence with which everyone back at McMurdo Sound regarded his audacious plan, had no desire to turn back now.

Leaving the heaviest sledge behind, they began to inch their way up the slope, zig-zagging to reduce the angle as they climbed. Slowly they moved higher and higher and higher, until the vehicles could go no more—Hillary later described the feeling as being 'like flies clinging to the wall'.[7] Jettisoning another sledge, they crawled forward and upwards. It was 'touch and go',[8] but finally, with great relief, they inched their way to the top and on to a flat snow landing. Unhitching the sledges, they drove back down the slope and, retrieving the ones they had left behind, repeated the process.

There was still no sign of the dog teams that evening, and the next day Hillary could bear it no longer. He and Mulgrew set off in the Weasel down the glacier to search for them. Ten kilometres down, they turned off the motor and listened. Far in the distance came the wonderful sound of a man yelling commands to his dogs. By that evening all the men were together again. It was remarkable how quickly the dog teams were able to skim over the crevasse areas and climb the steep slopes. It was the weather, not the terrain, that had caused them to fall so far behind.

The dogs were of particular help the next day. The visibility was terrible, but the dog teams left tracks behind that the tractors could follow, always conscious of crevasse areas, which not infrequently loomed to the left and right. The surface began to change, a victim of intense winds rushing down the Staircases. Large sastrugi lay before them. Some were so high that the men had to be careful not to capsize as they drove over the peaks and tipped down the other side.

The fierce katabatic winds returned to challenge them over the following days. With the freezing temperatures and poor visibility making life so difficult, there was huge relief when eventually the visibility cleared and the men saw, away in the distance, a tiny black dot—the beginnings of the Plateau Depot that had been laid the previous autumn.

The vehicles had made it on to the Plateau! Even for a man who had conquered the world's tallest mountain, and may be supposed to take adventure in his stride, the feeling of success that Ed had in establishing a route up on to the Plateau was momentous:

> I climbed out of the Weasel trying to wipe the smirk of satisfaction off my face … I had some difficulty in concealing my considerable emotions. To see our four battered vehicles and the laden sledges at the Plateau Depot seemed to be the fulfilment of an impossible dream. I don't think that ever before, even on the summit of Everest, had I felt a greater sense of achievement.[9]

A few days earlier Ayres and Carlyon, together with two teams of dogs, had been flown up to the Polar Plateau, and they gave Hillary and his men a rousing welcome. It had taken two and a half weeks, but Hillary, Mulgrew, Ellis, Bates and Balham had overcome the forebodings of their Scott Base colleagues and achieved what many had believed to be impossible.

Miller and Marsh, however, with their dogs, had been forced to remain hunkered down in the blizzard winds. Finally, on the same day as the vehicles made it to the Plateau Depot, they were able to set off up the glacier again. Pushing their way through the wind and poor visibility, three days later they were reunited with the rest of the team.

'To see our four battered vehicles and the laden sledges at the Plateau Depot seemed to be the fulfilment of an impossible dream. I don't think that ever before, even on the summit of Everest, had I felt a greater sense of achievement.'

ED HILLARY

FOLLOWING PAGES: Close-up views of the Tucker Sno-Cat used by Vivian Fuchs on the crossing of Antarctica. The vehicle is on display at Canterbury Museum.

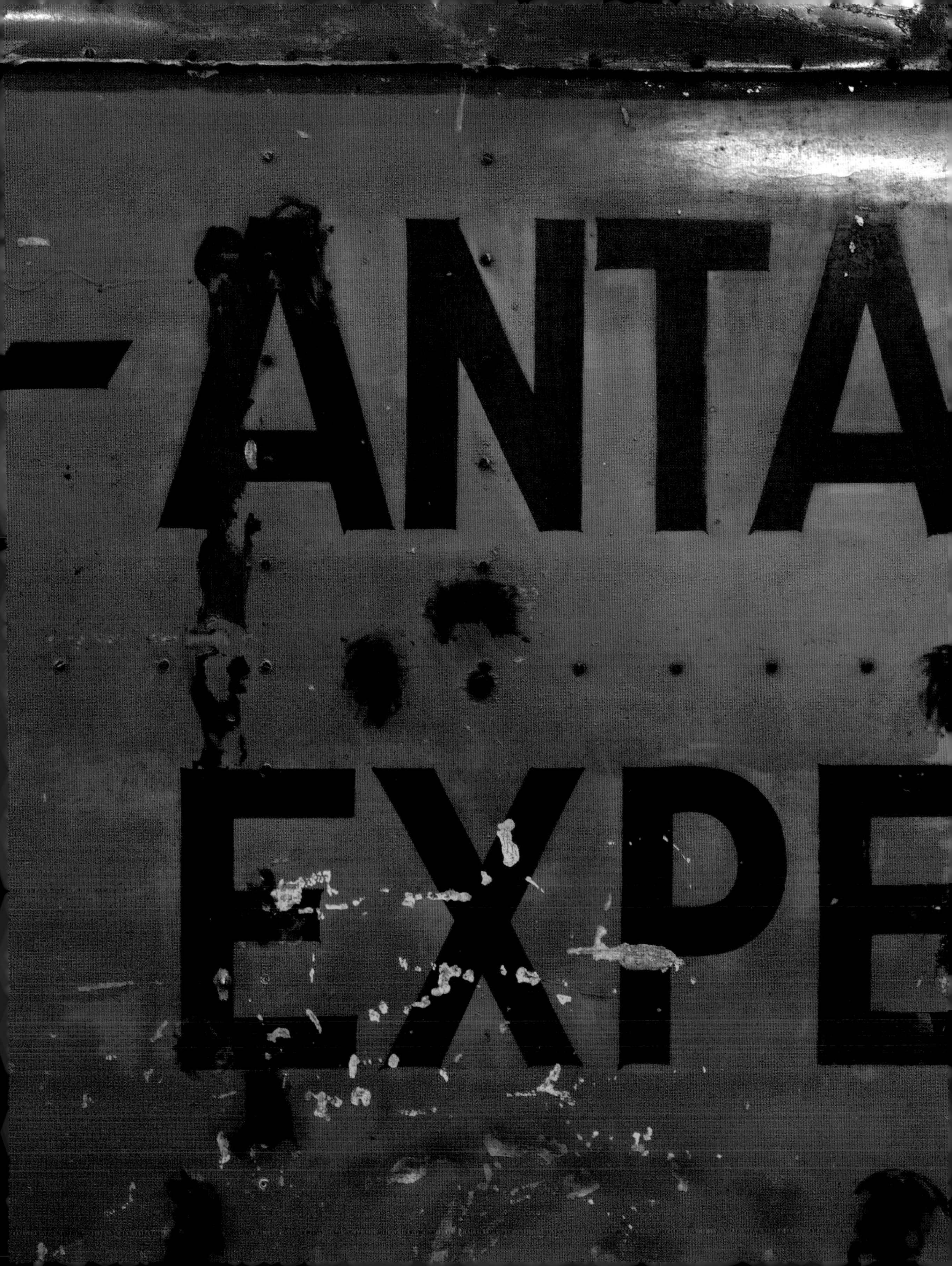
ANTA
EXPE

One of the Ferguson tractors
with the caboose attached.

Working together over the following week, with frequent deliveries by Claydon and Cranfield in the Beaver aircraft, the men fully stocked the Plateau Depot with supplies for Fuchs' crossing party. With that task complete, they turned their attention to the next stage.

Hillary had spent considerable time thinking and planning ahead. His stated goal, when he departed from Scott Base, had been to drive the vehicles to the South Geomagnetic Pole, where a gravity survey would be carried out. Earlier plans, which had involved a tractor trip to the Geographic South Pole,[10] had been publicly shelved when Hillary had received firm instructions from the Ross Sea Committee that his role was to support the TAE crossing party by establishing depots, and that he was not to attempt a run on the South Pole. This did not sit well with Hillary. Not only did he have ambitions to travel to

the South Pole, but he also wanted to give his men the opportunity to carry out significant surveying and geological fieldwork.

Despite the fetters being placed on him by the management committees in Wellington and London, over the Antarctic winter Hillary had quietly decided not to limit his plans. As he was to acknowledge in his official account of the expedition,

> … I have never suffered direction easily. Inevitably I came to regard the [Ross Sea] committee as one of my heavier burdens — while the committee developed a healthy suspicion of my actions which resulted in constant efforts (somewhat in vain, I fear) to exert a moderating brake.[11]

Now that Hillary had surmounted the considerable hurdle of the Skelton Glacier, he cast aside the stated plan of travelling to the South Geomagnetic

Pole. His reasons for doing this were expressed pragmatically. There was insufficient petrol for such a long, unsupported trip, and he had come to the conclusion that the tractors, and not the dogs, should be the main focus for establishing the next depot to support the crossing party. Hillary would concentrate, for now, on establishing the required depots for Fuchs' TAE crossing party.

The next stage of the journey was the establishment of a depot of supplies at 80°S, 148°E. Some 480 miles (approximately 770 kilometres) from Scott Base, it became known as Depot 480. This was consistent with Fuchs' instruction to 'establish a depot at 500 or as near thereto as is practicable'.[12] The men spent nearly two weeks at Plateau Depot before leaving on their journey to this next depot. In that time there were some changes in personnel, and two occasions on which the nature of the expedition suddenly took an unexpected turn.

On 3 November, while doing some paperwork inside the caboose, Ed was startled by sudden and frightening news. Bates came rushing over yelling that Ellis had been run over by a tractor. The outlook was grim. Ellis was lying face down on the ice. The tractor loomed above him, its large back wheels—encased in rubber tracks with metal cross-cleats—mere feet from his body. Ayres, with a horrified look on his face, was clambering down from the driver's seat.

Ed rushed over to Ellis, kneeling down beside his friend, his mind racing with thoughts of horrific damage to internal organs. Feeling sick with fear, he was relieved to see that Ellis was not only conscious but highly irritated by all the fuss. He explained that he had twisted his back while straining to lift up the drawbar on the tractor and, as a consequence, had felt a sudden weakness in his legs and collapsed on the ground. An old sports injury, he said; he was sure that he would recover. He was evacuated back to base, where he was advised to remain in bed for a couple of weeks.

Ed needed to find another driver, and his only prospect at that stage was Derek Wright, a cameraman who had been part of the Scott Base team the previous summer and had proven himself to be a resourceful and capable driver. The only problem was that Wright was in New Zealand. He was due to return to Scott Base that summer

to continue his filming, and with a little help once again from the Americans, Ed arranged for him to fly south two days later.

Derek Wright during the journey to the Pole.

Ellis' injury was not the only problem to be solved. A few days after his departure, the team suffered another blow. By this time there were only two men left at the Plateau Depot. The four dog teams and their drivers, Miller, Marsh, Ayres and Carlyon, had already departed on the journey to D480. Ed and Balham had flown back to Scott Base, the former to catch up with happenings there and the latter to pursue his biological study of seals. Less than two months later Balham was to lead a scientific expedition to explore a part of the Dry Valleys. Meanwhile, Bates and Mulgrew remained at the lonely outpost, busily preparing the vehicles and supplies for the next leg of the journey.

One day Mulgrew suffered a serious accident while climbing up on the roof of the caboose. In the cold and icy conditions, he slipped and fell, landing hard on the caboose's drawbar and breaking several ribs. This was a disaster for Mulgrew, who was desperate to continue with the journey over the Plateau, and for the driving team. Knowing that he had no choice but to evacuate Mulgrew back to Scott Base, Ed hoped that he would be well enough to fill in as radio operator, allowing Gawn, the current radio operator, to take

Murray Ellis' jacket from the expedition features
a stitched-on panel bearing his name. All members of
the New Zealand party were issued with these jackets,
so labels were a way of personalising clothing.

MURRAY ELLIS' JACKET

his place as driver. Unfortunately, Gawn had a terrible reputation as a driver, being known as an excellent destroyer of wheel tracks and generally getting his vehicles into difficult situations. He was, however, the only available replacement at the time.

Thirteen days after arriving up on the Polar Plateau, and after having successfully established Plateau Depot, the three tractors and the Weasel set off for D480. This time there were only four drivers: Hillary, Gawn, Bates and Wright. It was Hillary's turn to come down with the nasty bug that was making its way through each of the men, meaning enforced rests until he became well enough to return to the driving seat. The driving conditions were extremely boggy and this, coupled with the steady incline, meant the vehicles made very slow progress. The first day's driving resulted in a grand total of 7 kilometres travelled. It was four days before they made any real progress.

In addition to the difficult surface conditions, navigation was proving difficult. This was Ed's responsibility, and despite his experience he was making, in his words, 'a proper hash of it'.[13] It all came to a head four days after trudging away from Plateau Depot when they were forced to make a correction in the direction they were taking, effectively reducing the distance they had gained by almost 10 kilometres. Tempers were frayed, with Bates in particular envisaging endlessly wandering around the vast Polar Plateau.

Changes were made. The base plate of the astro-compass was tightened to prevent the vibrations from the tractor causing it to pivot incorrectly, and Ed made a conscious decision to be extra careful with his mathematics when making the necessary calculations. Finally, the men decided to travel in the evening hours. At that time of the year the sun never sets at such latitude in the Antarctic, and travelling at this time had no significant drawbacks aside from the slightly lower temperatures caused by the sun being oriented to the south rather than the north. The major advantage, however, was that now the men would be travelling towards the sun and this made steering, while navigating with a sun compass, that much easier.

During the regular radio sessions they had with Scott Base, word had come through that Fuchs was making slow progress towards the Pole. Hillary began to wonder whether Fuchs' party, now much behind schedule, would be able to complete its journey in time to catch the last ship out of McMurdo Sound in autumn. But they had their own job to do. The surface was becoming progressively harder, which was a good thing, but with this hardness came the dreaded sastrugi. The towed sledges were battered and bruised by the constant lifting and crashing. Repairing the sledges became another endless task to undertake and endure.

Striking whiteout conditions, they kept doggedly on until eventually they had to admit defeat and wait until the visibility improved, after a 2-tonne sledge capsized over a giant sastrugi that was invisible in the murk.

Just one day out from D480, the travel took a disastrous turn. With only 29 kilometres to go, the men were pushing on quickly ahead. Hillary, driving the Weasel, and some distance behind the others, began to notice that the vehicles ahead of him were regularly breaking through the ice, leaving holes about a foot wide. He suddenly realised that they must be entering an area of crevasses, and tore off after the tractors as fast as he could, to warn them. On this occasion, however, Bates was unstoppable. Hillary raced around a hummock and slammed to a halt, nearly running into the last sledge of the last tractor. They were all stopped, in a rather stunned line, with the middle tractor on an odd angle. Bates' tractor, going fast, had crossed a crevasse and got

Guyon Warren inspects a large sastrugi on the edge of the Polar Plateau.

to the other side before the snow bridge collapsed, but the second tractor, with a pale Wright at the wheel, was not so lucky. One track was deeply imbedded in a crevasse.

The vehicles were caught in a very nasty area and were completely surrounded by crevasses of varying sizes. To effect a rescue, Ed nervously climbed on to Bates' tractor and carefully manoeuvred it, picking his way cautiously, until it too sat with the third tractor and the Weasel on the other side of the crevasse. The only chance of extricating the stricken tractor was for all three of the other vehicles to pull at once. After much manoeuvring and organising of sledges, constant checks on the stability of the ice beneath them, and many wasted hours, all three vehicles were finally roped up to the stricken tractor. On Ed's signal, they all accelerated at once and, with a sudden jerk, the tractor was wrenched free. The force of the movement caused a huge amount of the damaged snow bridge to collapse and the men stared in horror at a hole as large as a house, with sheer sides, of monstrous depth and hungry enough to swallow a hundred Fergusons.[14]

The rather subdued group was forced to backtrack several kilometres before trying a slightly different direction in the hope of skirting around the treacherous crevasse area. Slowly their confidence returned and they gradually increased speed and were once more making good progress

'...the black dots in the unlimited expanse of the Plateau were as welcome a sight to the pilot as the aircraft was to those waiting below.'

JOHN CLAYDON

until telltale cracks began to appear again. Bates, reprising his role as the lead tractor driver, felt his vehicle sink a little and he pulled to a stop shortly afterwards. Once again, the ability of Fergusons to find crevasses could not be faulted. The snow bridge that Bates had just driven over had barely held his weight and was now partially collapsed. The crevasse, which was about 2.5 metres wide, was bottomless and currently lay, like some kind of nasty joke, between the lead tractor and the other vehicles. By this time the men were absolutely exhausted, and they decided that the most sensible course was to set up camp and have a sleep. Even pitching a tent was a problem—after choosing what appeared to be a safe place, they realised, with a little digging, that half the tent was erected over a gaping chasm!

Refreshed after a decent sleep, and with a good deal of investigation of the surrounding area, they placed flags marking a relatively safe route ahead through the crevasses. The main problem was getting the remaining two tractors and the Weasel across the weak snow bridge to Bates' tractor. In Ed's words, they took 'a bit of a risk',[15] as, each hitched firmly to the lead tractor, they sped the remaining vehicles across.

Finally, on 25 November, thirteen days after leaving Plateau Depot, they made it to the site of the new depot, D480. Three days later the four dog teams, and their drivers, Miller, Marsh, Ayres

and Carlyon, joined them. Another welcome arrival was Claydon and the little Beaver aircraft, which touched down on their makeshift landing strip on 29 November. It is a long flight from Scott Base, over the Ross Ice Shelf, up the Skelton Glacier and several hundred kilometres over the Polar Plateau. The wind and visibility can change at any time, making flying treacherous and attempting a landing even more so. As Claydon commented in his report:

> Reaching D480 presented a navigational problem ... During the latter stages of this flight to the Depot, the trail party nonchalantly mentioned over the radio that they had fixed their position more accurately five or so miles away from the previous point. In striking contrast to the white desert below the air was 'blue' for miles. As can well be imagined the black dots in the unlimited expanse of the Plateau were as welcome a sight to the pilot as the aircraft was to those waiting below.[16]

The plane brought supplies, a large bag of mail and a very happy Ellis. His back now healed, he had come to relieve Gawn of his tractor duties. An equally happy Gawn boarded the plane to fly back to Scott Base. On another aerial visit a couple of days later the plane delivered Mulgrew to the Plateau. Ed was particularly pleased to see his old friend, who he counted on as his most staunch and

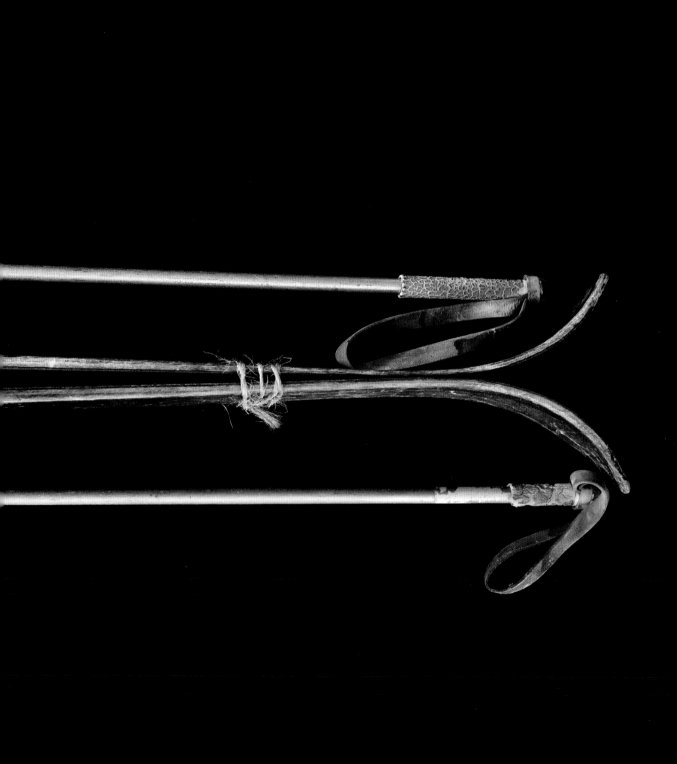

BOB MILLER'S SKIS AND POLES

Ed Hillary on a Ferguson tractor leaving
Depot 480 in December 1957.

willing supporter.[17] The 'Old Firm', as the four who had made the trip to Cape Crozier were named, was back together.

With bad weather, it took nine days to establish D480. Following agreement from Fuchs to lay yet another depot, the next major leg of the journey was to establish D700, a depot 700 miles (1126 kilometres) from Scott Base. An extra tractor driver was press-ganged into service with the arrival of Douglas McKenzie, the expedition's press correspondent, who had flown to the Plateau to spend, so he thought, a couple of days with the men.

It was a cheerful crew who set off from D480 into perfect weather and good surface conditions. Ed was contemplating that they might, at the good rate they were travelling, make it to D700 in five days. If they could do that, surely it was entirely possible to travel just another 500 miles and drive all the way to the Pole? From the very earliest days of planning with Fuchs, Hillary had expressed his view that the New Zealand team should have enough food and fuel to enable it to drive to the South Pole if possible. As noted, during the previous winter at Scott Base he had publicly changed his ambition to that of reaching the South Geomagnetic Pole, thinking it prudent to curtail his plans due to, as he put it, 'much expressed and unexpressed opposition to my making any effort to get to the South Pole'.[18] In April 1957, Guyon Warren had recorded a less politic view of the differing interests playing out during the Scott Base winter:

> Wind of the proposed attempt by tractors to the Pole from here, has got to England and upset the TAE management committee very badly, thinking of the horrid possibility of us getting there and not Fuchs' party. As a result Bowden [the chairman of the Ross Sea Committee] has been tackled, and he has more or less forbidden Ed to try, so now plans have turned round to the Geomagnetic Pole (which isn't the South Magnetic Pole) where the Russians have an IGY base. It is about 78S, 110E and 1000 tractor miles from here. It is called Vostok.[19]

Now, nearly eight months later, with thoughts of the South Geomagnetic Pole abandoned, and determinedly chugging their way towards D700, the South Pole was undoubtedly a glittering, perhaps now attainable, prize. They were making fantastic time, and broke their own record for distance travelled in one day: 52 miles (84 kilometres). The Polar Plateau was not, however, going to let them get away with it too easily.

Three days after leaving D480 they were within 160 kilometres of D700, and they unloaded some supplies at a small depot, called Midway Depot, that was to be used by the dog teams (and by Fuchs' crossing party if necessary). Large sastrugi were becoming increasingly regular. Small crevasses littered the area. The Weasel began to labour badly and the men suspected that it would not last much longer. Still they pushed on, and then quite suddenly they realised that the small crevasses were no longer small; they were nasty, large, sheer-sided beasts with dark depths that ran at different angles to each other. At one point, so tight was the angle being asked of a tractor and its load that the track caught on the drawbar of the sledge and broke. This was a moment of dread. The tractor was caught in the middle of two large crevasses and could not be moved until the track was repaired.

Hillary was hugely thankful for the 'courage and determination' of Ellis and Bates,[20] who worked for hours in the frigid conditions, all the while perched on the edges of deadly chasms, to painstakingly repair the damage. The terrifying game of Russian roulette endured after the tractor was repaired. Although the men had investigated, and marked, a route through the crevasses there was, as Hillary recalled, simply no way of avoiding them:

> We then started winding our way over the flagged route. It was a tiring and worrying procedure, for every new bridge was a new gamble and we never really knew when we mightn't strike the jackpot. By the time we had come to the end of our flagged route there was a series of gaping holes behind us and I think all of us were noticing the strain.[21]

It took eight hours to travel through less than 5 kilometres of crevasses. It was all too much for the Weasel. After sickening for some time, it finally gave up. There was no choice but to abandon it.

One of the Ferguson tractors caught in a crevasse.

The team began to make quite good progress again, but they missed the company of the Weasel, and its soft snow speciality, when the Fergusons became endlessly bogged in unwelcome softer conditions. On and on the team plodded until, within 16 kilometres of D700, a slow-motion horror played out. A snow bridge gave way and the tractor, with Bates driving, sank. At the last moment, the ends of the cab caught on the edge of the crevasse and stopped it just before what had seemed an inevitable plummet. Bates, badly shaken, clambered out of the tractor and climbed back up to the surface. The thought of losing another vehicle so soon after the demise of the Weasel was deeply worrying.

The tractor was tilted on an angle with its front wheels higher than the back. Securing it by ropes to ensure it did not fall further, the men began to

dig, clearing away the ice until they had fashioned a steep ramp down to the tractor's front wheels. They hoped that, by securing tow ropes to the front of the tractor, they could haul it up the ramp and out of the crevasse. There remained one further obstacle. The tractor was still in gear. Mulgrew climbed down to it and entered the cab, working quickly to put in into neutral. His friends watched tensely as the tractor lurched a few inches downwards with his weight before he was able to scramble back out again.

Using two tractors and tow ropes in unison, the men knew that there would be only one chance to pull it out. If it did not work the first time, the tractor would be dislodged from its tentative hold and fall backwards into the hole, with no hope of retrieving it. Hillary and Ellis together surged their tractors forward. Hillary was almost jerked out of his seat as the tension on the tow rope bit with the sudden weight. Thinking that the rope must have broken, he looked behind him and was delighted to see that the tractor had been wrested from its hole and dragged up the rough ramp.

It was a happy and relieved group of men who ground the last few kilometres to D700. The Plateau put on some extra-soft conditions, forcing them to relay their loads and robbing them of a final speedy flourish to this part of their journey.

Ed Hillary, Jim Bates and George Marsh at Plateau Depot.

Nevertheless, they had made it safely, and they received a warm welcome from their old friends Marsh and Miller, who had arrived two days earlier, together with their raucous dog teams.

For Ed, the establishment of D700 was a significant milestone:

> In a way D700 meant the end of our major task. It was the last depot for Bunny Fuchs—almost the reason why our expedition had originally started. To reach it in such force and in reasonably good time seemed to justify all our effort and our plans.[22]

The stocking of D700 took five days with the assistance of the Beaver. Hillary sent a message to Fuchs informing him that the New Zealanders had established D700 and would now attempt to travel to the South Pole. Controversy ensued. Fuchs' progress on the other side of the continent had been relatively slow up to this point, and his expedition was unlikely to reach the Pole until the New Year.

McKenzie, the press correspondent who had joined the crew between D480 and D700, aware that he was in danger of neglecting his reporting responsibilities, now flew back to Scott Base. The remaining drivers—Hillary, Ellis, Mulgrew, Bates and Wright—left D700 on 20 December 1957 heading south, now 550 miles (885 kilometres) from the Pole. They had carefully considered the

Peter Mulgrew rests for a moment outside a tent at D700.

supplies that they needed and had discarded anything superfluous. They carried enough fuel to get them to the Pole, with no reserves. If the fuel ran low, Ed planned to drop one vehicle and continue on with only two. They also took a man-hauling sledge. In the event of complete failure of the vehicles, or loss of all fuel, they would even walk the last 100 miles to the Pole.

While at Plateau Depot, Ellis and Bates had expressed their reluctance to take the vehicles past D700. They believed that the tractors would be worn out and that it was risky to drive beyond the supporting range of the Beaver. By the time they reached D700 the two men were less worried, but they could hardly be described as enthusiastic about continuing. In contrast, Ed was firm in his determination to reach the South Pole, but even so the perilous nature of the task he was imposing upon the group weighed heavily:

> I left with mixed feelings—doubts of the unknown; fear of crevasses; a deep-seated worry about our petrol supplies; and a little voice in the back of my mind saying, 'Do you think you can find the South Pole?' These were counterbalanced by a vast confidence in my companions' abilities to keep the wheels rolling, plus an over-riding conviction that we'd get there come hell or high water.[23]

During the next scheduled radio contact with Scott Base, further pressure bore down upon Ed when he received a message from the Ross Sea Committee that he was not to proceed beyond D700. Hillary's reaction was practical but certainly not politic:

> If an explorer in the field always waited for permission from his committee at home then nothing would get done or it would be done too late. Time spent sitting around at depots was just time wasted. With a grunt I put the message aside…[24]

After travelling for weeks up on the Polar Plateau, removed and isolated from the machinations of human expectations and monetary and political demands, and utterly dependent upon himself and a small group for the daily essentials in order to survive, Ed was able to be so pragmatic. A successful conclusion to this expedition would,

however, inevitably shatter the isolation. The resulting groundswell of recriminations and criticisms would be impossible to ignore.

Now, though, it was crevasses that were causing problems. They were a constant threat and the men made careful and slow progress at times, meticulously marking the route with flags for their own safety but also so that Fuchs' team, on its way north, would have a way through. Eventually their luck ran out. Ellis, in the lead tractor, missed one of the flags by about 30 metres and, although the following tractor came across safely, the caboose came to grief. Swinging sickeningly above an enormous, dark cavern, the caboose dangled by its tow bar at one end, and at the other by the wire rope that attached it to the sledges behind. The crevasse was so vast that it extended, on all sides, below the poled route that the men had just driven over. Rather as they had done when they rescued Bates' tractor, the men resorted to digging an ice ramp down to the caboose's ski runners and, using three tractors pulling at once, heaved it out.

Christmas Day, when it came, was full of cheer. Ellis, showing admirable forethought, treated each of the men to a tot of brandy that he had hauled all the way from Scott Base. Salmon fishcakes, tinned peaches, hot cocoa and fruitcake made a delicious Christmas dinner. On Boxing Day, Hillary sent to Scott Base the message that was to become famous:

> We are heading hell-bent for the Pole,
> God willing and crevasses permitting.[25]

The following day, Hillary received an urgent message from Fuchs requesting him to establish a further fuel depot and abandon his plan of driving to the Pole. Ed was stunned. This was the first he had heard about Fuchs being concerned about fuel supplies, although in light of the slow progress Fuchs was making it perhaps should not have been a surprising request. For Ed, the abandonment of the remaining journey to the Pole was not an option. He and his men had only enough fuel to drive on to the Pole or to return to D700. They could not sit at their current position and give their fuel to Fuchs, when he eventually arrived, given that Fuchs was still about a month away. They simply did not have the food to wait that long. Ed's reply was direct and non-apologetic.

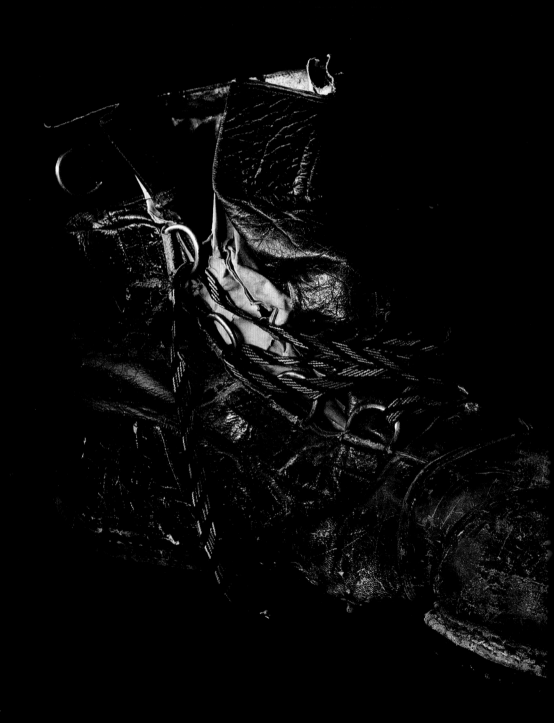

The black leather padded boots with mesh insoles worn by Ed Hillary during the Trans-Antarctic Expedition. These are now part of Canterbury Museum's collection.

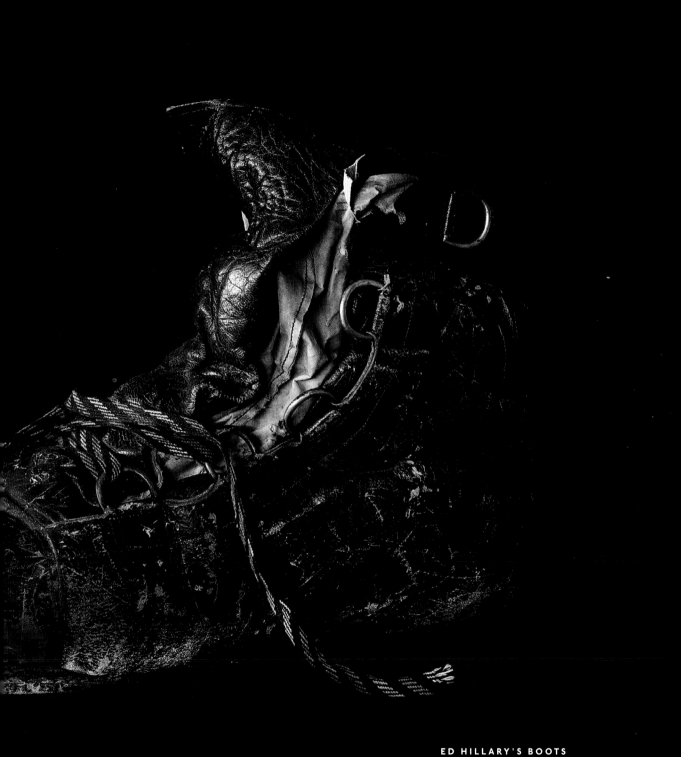

ED HILLARY'S BOOTS

In Hillary's mind, Fuchs' message had come too late. He was going to push on to the Pole. To safeguard Fuchs' party, he arranged for extra fuel to be flown to D700 and he reminded Fuchs that, in an emergency, some fuel would be able to be obtained from the American base at the Pole.

As Hillary's team continued south into the thin air and freezing conditions, now 3000 metres above sea level, the tractors laboured mightily. It was a constant, weary fight to keep them from stalling. This sort of travel made the vehicles hungry for fuel and, feeling nervous pressure about finding the most direct route, Ed strived to take accurate readings. He was very aware that his navigation had been far from faultless up to that point, and was dismayed to find that one of his pieces of equipment, a bubble sextant, was becoming more inaccurate the higher they climbed. At times, too, the sun was obscured by low, thick fog, so that it was impossible to use it as a guide.

The ground conditions became steadily worse, reducing the vehicles to a slow, hesitant crawl so that they required constant digging out. Coupled with the navigation problems, it seemed that the closer they came to the Pole, the more elusive it became. Thoughts of driving in endless circles, eventually running out of fuel and being forced to walk, now loomed, not as distant fantasy, but as an approaching reality. Eventually, the team was brought to a stop. The tractors, even pulling the sledges in unison, simply could not move forward in the deep snow.

The men decided on a drastic step: they would abandon all reserves that were not vitally necessary. Leaving behind two sledges, 80 days' worth of rations, kerosene, the man-hauling sledge, emergency tents, camping gear and numerous other items, they both lightened the load and conserved fuel. They slowly set off again. The pace was still agonisingly slow but at least they were now making some progress. Yet the fuel consumption remained too high, and with a great deal of reluctance they resorted to abandoning all their heavy tractor spare parts and tools.

By 2 January 1958, Hillary and his men had about 112 kilometres (70 miles) to go. Although the fastest that they were able to go, intermittently, was only 3 miles per hour, at least the progress was steady. The major problem was still fuel. The

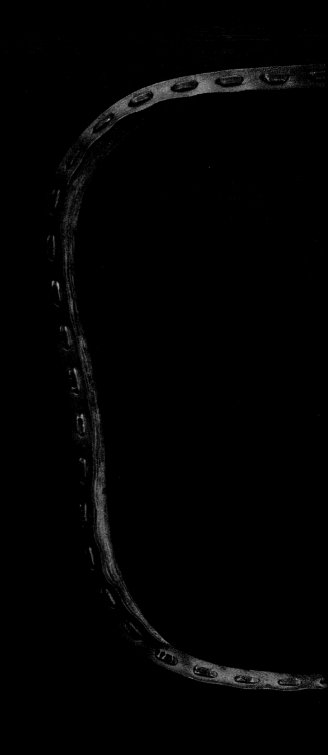

Bob Miller, George Marsh and their dog teams had been reunited with Ed at D700, before Hillary and his team continued south towards the Pole.

BOB MILLER'S DOG WHIP

'I remember the warmth of the welcome from our American friends. One said, "You're probably hungry. Would you like a steak meal?" We said, "We sure would."'

ED HILLARY

hunger of the tractors, as they ground through the soft snow, was immense. At this rate, the best that could be hoped was that they would inch their way to the Pole with a gallon, maybe two, to spare.

The men were exhausted. It was time to finish this journey. Waking up to a murky, windy day, they decided to keep driving, without stopping to camp, until they reached the Pole. For 24 hours they trudged on and on, stopping occasionally for a brief break before clambering aboard again and plodding on.

News came through from Fuchs that he was still over 600 kilometres from the Pole. This hardly cheered the men. Ed, worrying constantly about his navigation and the distinct possibility of missing the Pole, kept checking his instruments and peering out for any sign of the American base. A tiny black dot, far away in the distance, stubbornly stayed put despite his blinking and looking again. Excitedly he turned his tractor towards it. A flag! There was a line of them, perhaps marking the airstrip of the South Pole base.

A much happier group of men that evening, they set up camp and made radio contact with Scott Base. Aware that there was huge media interest in their progress, and that radio waves were hardly confidential, a codeword had been prearranged for when they were within sight of the South Pole. The London *Times* and the BBC were financially supporting the TAE, including the New Zealand party, and they needed to be the first to know. Mulgrew turned the radio on and uttered the single codeword: 'rhubarb'. The exhausted men settled down into their sleeping bags and slept.

The last 15 kilometres of the journey must have felt as if they took forever. The fog and murk of the previous day had disappeared, leaving a pristine, sunny day, but, stubbornly holding out to the end, the tractors could not make rapid progress in the soft snow. Finally, crawling to the finish line, they were there! The welcome at the South Pole on 4 January 1958 was warm, cheerful and busy, with cameras, handshakes and congratulations all round.

Half a century on, recounting his arrival at the Pole Station, Hillary noted that 'it was quite thrilling for us. I remember the warmth of the welcome from our American friends. One said, "You're probably hungry. Would you like a steak meal?" We said, "We sure would."'[26]

Sir Edmund Hillary, Jim Bates, Murray Ellis, Derek Wright and Peter Mulgrew were thrilled to have finally finished their long, cold and at times frightening journey. It had taken just under three months, and they had covered just over 2000 kilometres, from ignominious beginnings on the Ross Ice Shelf, to the terrifyingly steep ascents up the Skelton, to narrow escapes from horrendous crevasses and wallowing in soul-destroying soft snow.

There was no doubt now. Three tractors and five men had the tenacity, skill and luck, not only to go beyond the Ross Ice Shelf but to be the first overland expedition, since Captain Scott and his men in 1912, to travel to the South Pole. But, in stark contrast to Scott and his party, who had to turn for home in a race for their survival, Hillary's team could now relax. Settling down at South Pole Station they stretched out their weary bodies and watched a western movie.[27]

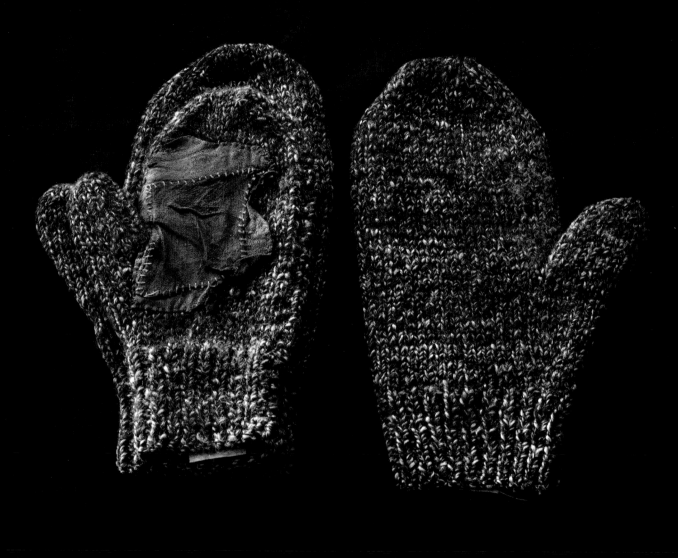

All the men on the expedition wore mittens in the cold conditions. This set of three was hand-knitted for Guyon Warren by his wife, Sally, using wool that originally came from a jersey. There was only enough wool to create three mittens, so the smaller one on the left was worn inside the larger mitten. These are now part of Canterbury Museum's collection.

GUYON WARREN'S MITTENS

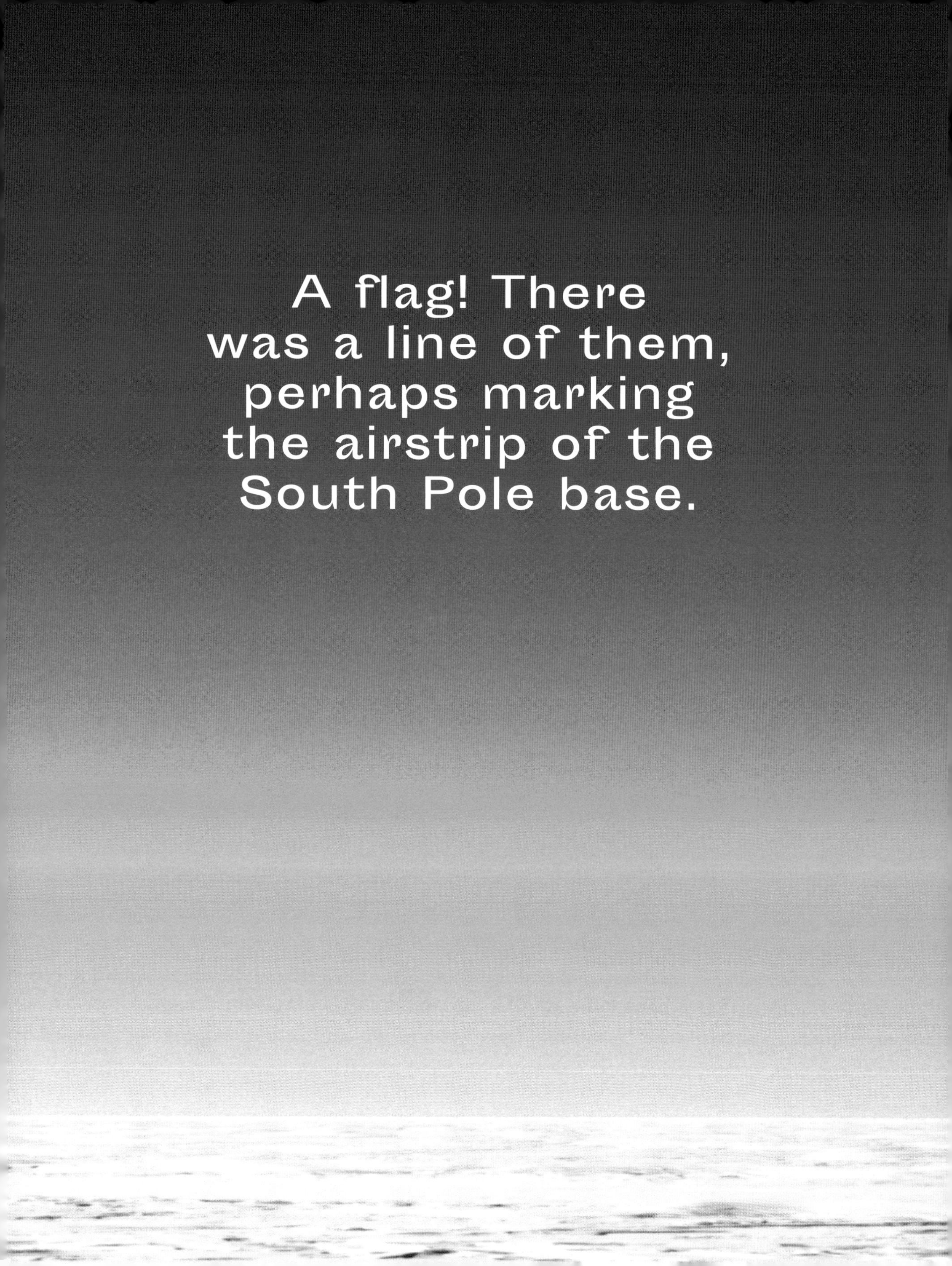

A flag! There
was a line of them,
perhaps marking
the airstrip of the
South Pole base.

The hardworking Joe, one of the sledging dogs.

DOGS

ON THE PLATEAU

SIX

'Oh for some sunshine … today was just as miserable as sledging can be.'[1] Fortunately, the following morning, Bob Miller and George Marsh ended the climb out of the Skelton Glacier and on to the vast Polar Plateau. It had taken them twelve long days to scale the glacier.[2]

Waiting for them to arrive were the tractor party (Sir Edmund Hillary, Jim Bates, Peter Mulgrew, Murray Ellis and Ron Balham) and also two teams of dogs led by Harry Ayres and Roy Carlyon. The latter two had been flown up to the Plateau from Scott Base and were to join Miller and Marsh on the next leg of their journey.

Over the next six days the men worked to establish Plateau Depot for Fuchs and the TAE crossing party. On 8 November 1957, nearly a

week later and with the depot now complete, the dog drivers were free to go. Trouble struck immediately. The fully laden sledges were simply too heavy for the dogs to haul. Less than 2 kilometres on, Miller abandoned his survey gear and the whole party offloaded a significant quantity of both man and dog rations and kerosene for the tractors to pick up. They set off again. The surface was horrendous, with a sandy, gripping texture, and after travelling only just over 10 kilometres the dogs were absolutely exhausted.[3]

It was a bitter blow. At this rate, they would never be able to make it to the next depot, D480, which they were tasked to help establish. The men had dedicated countless hours to training their dogs during the preceding winter. If the surface

A hand-drawn illustration that appears in Harry Ayres'
notebook on training sled dogs. The book was gifted

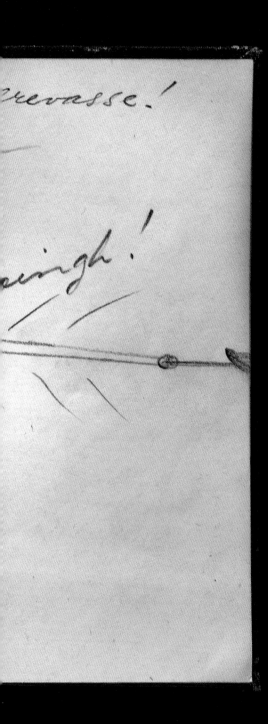

conditions continued to be this difficult, the training would all have been for nothing. They agreed to carry on until the tractors caught up with them, and then decide what to do. Ayres, a mountain guide and a determined, dedicated dog driver, reflected in a somewhat understated fashion in his diary that they were all 'feeling upset'.[4]

Over the following few days the ground conditions remained bad but eventually, five days later, the surface became easier. In order to avoid the terrifying crevasses of the upper Mulock Glacier, one of the largest of the giant glaciers draining the Plateau, the first few days of travel were not south but north-west and west. Ironically, despite all their efforts to date, although they were many metres higher in altitude on the Plateau, their latitude was the same as the head of the Skelton Glacier, just 16 kilometres south of Scott Base.

Just as the surface conditions improved, drama struck. Miller fell into a crevasse as he was in the process of placing one of his exhausted dogs on to the still-moving sledge for a rest. First one foot, and then the other, went through the snow. Miller hurled himself backwards, spreading his arms wide, as he fell in up to his waist. Oblivious, the dogs kept pulling the sledge and it sailed over and away from the crevasse. Turning on to his stomach, Miller clawed his way out of the hole and rapidly crawled away.[5] Ayres, coming up behind him, looked down the hole and stared in amazement. If Miller had not managed to stop himself he would 'have gone down to eternity',[6] for the hole stretched at least 30 metres down, its bottom somewhere far below that, hidden by the darkness.

That evening, the men warned the tractor party over the radio of the crevasses, although the tractors were still some way behind them, floundering in the awful, sticky conditions that had beset the dog drivers after they had left the last depot.

Nine days after leaving Plateau Depot, the four men celebrated the 100-mile (160-kilometre) mark. It had not been easy and more difficulties were to follow. For three days a blizzard forced them to a stop and they were confined to tents. Marsh, who had shared a tent up the Skelton Glacier with Miller, was now struck down with the same nasty flu-like virus that had flattened his tent-mate. He was not in any state to travel.

The arduous conditions had taken their toll. Travelling south, and away from the sun, the men's faces had not felt its warmth for three weeks. They were not only physically exhausted but were also suffering from frostbite on their noses and cheeks.

When they were finally able to break camp and set off again some days later, there was a bizarre heat wave. The rising temperatures brought on snowfalls that obliterated all visibility. No sun, no horizon, just impenetrable white. The men had to be very careful to keep all four teams close together. In the swirling wind, sledge tracks made by the leading teams were quickly obscured and they failed to find the tracks left by the tractors, which had by now overtaken them.

With no visible sun, navigation was difficult. They had to rely on the box compass and their calculations of the magnetic variation this near to the South Pole. Close to their destination and not realising that the tractor party, by now at D480, was having similar difficulties with navigation, they blindly drove their dogs on. Ascending a steep hump about 30 metres above the surrounding area, Marsh paused for a moment and peered into the distance. Far away, to the east, there was more visibility. Straining to focus, he saw a thin black line. It was the tractor party at D480. The dog teams had passed the depot and were now forced to make a 90-degree turn and travel for several miles before reuniting with Hillary and his crew. As luck would have it, the tracks that the dogs and their sledges left would play a valuable role a few days later.[7]

The arduous conditions had taken their toll. Travelling south, and away from the sun, the men's faces had not felt its warmth for three weeks. They were not only physically exhausted but were also suffering from frostbite on their noses and cheeks. But the work had to go on, and the men of both teams spent the next few days preparing for the next leg of their journey and, with the Beaver arrivals, unloading supplies to stock D480.

Some significant changes to the teams' plans were also being made, with Ed giving voice to his intention of going all the way to the South Pole. Miller was noticeably cool about the idea and, in some exasperation, expressed his opposition to it while at D480: 'This Pole Dash of Ed's which he now informs me is officially on. I can't see any justifiable point in it.'[8] Another change was that the four dog teams were to be split back into two pairs. Now confident that the tractors were reliable and capable of travelling along the Plateau to the next planned depot, Ed agreed that one pair of dog teams could be released from the TAE plan and be free to carry out exploratory work. As a consequence, Ayres and Carlyon headed east from D480 to survey the area at the head of the Darwin Glacier, with the intention of descending it to the Ross Ice Shelf.

GEORGE MARSH AND BOB MILLER

Marsh and Miller, meanwhile, set out with twenty-five days of dog and man rations to reach the next, and last, depot to be established: D700. From there, the men would strike out towards the west to carry out surveying work. Leaving D480 on 1 December, with Miller still suffering from a sore throat, they travelled for a day before encountering nasty crevassed terrain. They noticed that small holes, or slots, were beginning to appear. Suddenly Marsh fell through. He grabbed hold of the side of his sledge and hauled himself out. Two of Miller's dogs also fell through at different times but, still bound by their harnesses, came to no harm.

It was, crevasses aside, a much more pleasant journey to D700 than it had been to D480. The weather was good, with many gloriously clear days, and Miller, now well in the rhythm of sledging life, began to enjoy himself:

> average just under 18 miles per day which is far beyond our expectation. But who knows we may yet have bad weather. Just endless plateau in every direction but still some undulations. The weather is almost inviting us to stop for a lunch break. As it is we sit down on the sunny side of our sledges and have a Thermos of cocoa and some chocolate.[9]

Bizarrely, on 8 December, when they were about 800 kilometres from McMurdo Sound, the men observed a lone skua gull flying above them. Apart from one that Ernest Shackleton had reported in the Beardmore Glacier area fifty years earlier,[10] this was a rarity—the bird was an incredible distance from its usual food sources along the coast. The only explanation appeared to be that it had been following the camping men for days, feasting on any leftovers and dog waste.

When they were about 160 kilometres beyond D480, the men built a cairn. This marked the site where they wished the tractor drivers to stock the small depot called Midway Depot, for their later use, along with some fuel for Fuchs' team.

Miller and Marsh, cheerfully, with a healthy respect for their dogs, and full of confidence in their own abilities, reached the site of D700 on 13 December. They had arrived well ahead of the tractor party and were rather bemused when, after three days, the tractors arrived with one less vehicle and one extra man. Miller and Marsh had left D480 before the arrival of Douglas McKenzie, the press correspondent, and were not aware that he had joined the tractor journey. With a journalist, and also a cameraman (Derek Wright), in the tractor party, Miller wryly noted, 'Ed is certainly watching his publicity.'[11]

The weather was proving difficult for flying and the enforced inactivity at D700 over a period of several days meant differing priorities came to the fore. Now that the last TAE depot had been successfully stocked, Miller wanted the dog teams to set off as soon as possible in order to undertake surveying work towards the south-east, in the Queen Alexandra Range. He was keen, however, for some fresh meat for the dogs and needed a forward depot established for this purpose.

Hillary, not wishing to forgo more than one drum of fuel, would not agree to using tractors for this, beyond a range of about 20 kilometres, and the only depot possibility was an airdrop. With an improvement in the weather and the arrival of the supplies by plane, Miller and Marsh, feeling rather chagrined, set off with their dogs. The plane was due to drop food to them in two days, by which time they would only have been able to travel 35 to 40 miles (56 to 64 kilometres) if the going was good. Ideally, a depot should have been a good deal further on in the journey, but on this occasion the sledges would have to be loaded up with the extra food at an early stage and the dogs forced to haul it. As expected, it was difficult for the dogs to haul the extra load and the next few days were a challenge.

By 21 December, three days out from D700 and with growing excitement, the men could see

CHOCOLATE

12 x 2.oz. BARS

SPECIALLY PACKED FOR
TRANS-ANTARCTIC EXPEDITION 1956
BY
ANDREW · LUSK & Cº LTD
LOND

This tin of chocolate bars, specially packed for the
Trans-Antarctic Expedition by Andrew Lusk & Co. Ltd of
London, is now part of Canterbury Museum's collection.

'The weather is almost inviting us to stop for a lunch break. As it is we sit down on the sunny side of our sledges and have a Thermos of cocoa and some chocolate.'

BOB MILLER

Another item that features in Canterbury Museum's collection is this chapstick in a metal case, made in Virginia and provided to members of the Trans-Antarctic Expedition.

LIP PROTECTION

mountain peaks, 160 kilometres away, pushing up out of the endless white flatness of the Plateau. Their excitement was tempered, unfortunately, by illness. Suffering from acute bowel pains, which they blamed on some tinned meat that had come in on the plane, they were forced to lie low for a couple of days.

Christmas Day dawned delightfully clear and sunny, with a friendly temperature and gentle breeze. The mountains were much closer now, beyond what appeared to be a line of nunataks, exposed peaks in a glacier, encouraging the men on. Christmas dinner was delicious—tinned frankfurters with mashed potato followed by a cocktail of brandy, lemon crystals, sugar and hot water.

By 27 December the men realised the nunataks were in fact a mountain range. This new discovery was later named the Queen Elizabeth Range after the expedition's patron. Back in the land of crevasses, they were careful about their route, and also fascinated by seeing rocks again. Not since leaving the Skelton Glacier had this been the case, the Polar Plateau being simply an endless expanse of ice. Immediately they set about surveying the area, whose mountains and glaciers stretched for miles.

Fortunately for Marsh, Bob Miller was not just a competent and keen surveyor but was also a handy, if previously inexperienced, dentist. Suffering from a sore front tooth, Marsh, the doctor, found himself in the position of patient. With Marsh lying down in the tent, resting his head on a makeshift pillow made from a ration box softened by down-filled pants, Miller worked to fill the hole in the tooth. Using a mirror as a mixing palette, he took great care in creating a temporary filling and he was rather justifiably proud of the end result.[12] One can only assume that Marsh was relieved it was just his tooth causing pain, not his appendix.

These men were extremely determined in their work. The surveying days were long and tiring, and always there were the lurking dangers inherent in mountain and crevasse work and the isolated nature of what they were undertaking. When they learned that they were expected back at D700 by early January, Miller refused to curtail the surveying programme, replying that they would be back by 18 January. They had come too far, and there was

so much work to be done. He was reluctant to leave until weather, time and supplies demanded it.

At their furthest point, before turning to head the dogs in the direction of D700, the men had travelled 1450 kilometres on their sledges. This does not take into account the 80 kilometres or more that they covered on foot in pursuit of their surveying and geological research. It was a remarkable achievement, but the job was not over yet. They returned to D700 two days earlier than planned, on 16 January. Incredibly, rather than arranging to be picked up by plane, the two men elected to drive their dog teams overland all the way back to Scott Base.

The return trip along the same route as they had travelled out on was made easier by being able to relax a little in terms of navigation. They now had tractor and dog tracks to follow and made very good progress, with the exception of some nasty autumnal blizzard winds that confined them to camp for four days and completely buried one of the dog teams. The temperatures were steadily dropping. The Antarctic summer is fleeting and the men knew that they needed to get off the Plateau rapidly.

By 8 February they were back at Plateau Depot after an absence of three months to the day, and a journey of 2060 kilometres. Their dogs were absolutely exhausted and they, and the men, rested for a couple of days before facing the descent of the Skelton Glacier. It took five days to descend what had taken them eleven to ascend. By 14 February Marsh and Miller were back at the Skelton Depot, and from there all that was left to face was the final sledge across the Ross Ice Shelf.

On the evening of 23 February 1958, after being away for 128 days, George Marsh and Bob Miller finally made it back to Scott Base. They had travelled to within 560 kilometres of the South Pole, surveyed and mapped entirely new mountain ranges, climbed to heights of 3300 metres, and amassed a significant geological collection of rock specimens which they hauled all the way back to Scott Base.

In travelling around 2700 kilometres, they had undertaken the longest dog sledging journey on record in Antarctica. It was an audacious, compelling and utterly courageous expedition by two Antarctic pioneers, and their wonderful dogs, and deserves to be remembered and respected as one of the truly great achievements of the New Zealand party of the Trans-Antarctic Expedition.

In travelling around 2700 kilometres, they had undertaken the longest dog sledging journey on record in Antarctica. It was an audacious, compelling and utterly courageous expedition by two Antarctic pioneers, and their wonderful dogs.

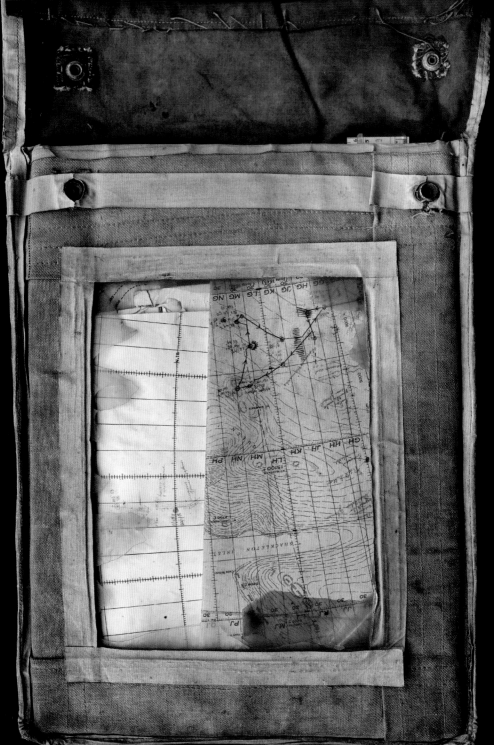

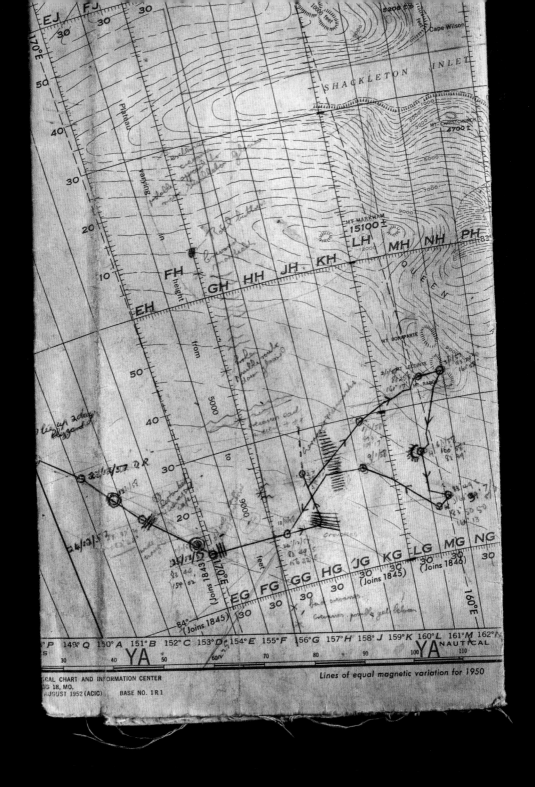

A portion of Bob Miller's map from his southern journey, after assisting with the establishment of D700.

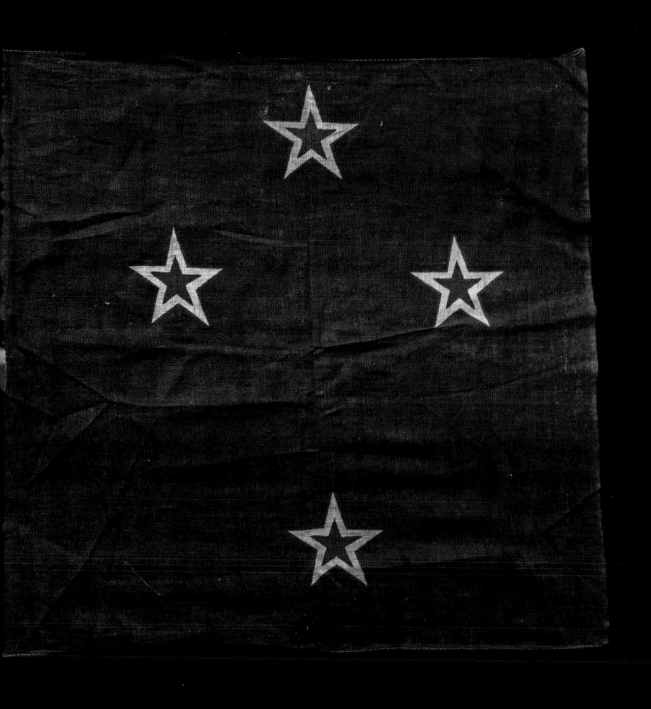

BOB MILLER'S NEW ZEALAND SLEDGING FLAG

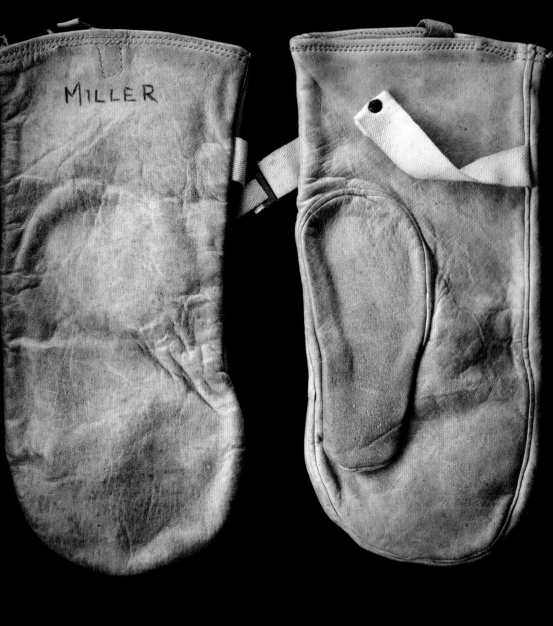

MILLER

The area that Ayres and Carlyon planned to survey was immense. Stretching from the Mulock Glacier in the north to the Byrd Glacier in the south, and down the Darwin Glacier to the Ross Ice Shelf, it was riddled with crevasses and nunataks. The Darwin Glacier, in particular, was a worrying hurdle. Taking the precaution of inspecting it by air before attempting its descent, Ayres was cautiously optimistic that it was navigable: 'I am impressed with the Darwin Glacier, we are going to have fun dodging ice all the way down and the crevasses are numerous [with] some quite shaky bridges over them.'[13]

Leaving D480 on 7 December, the men travelled east for three days and, with good ground conditions and favourable weather, covered over 120 kilometres. They set up a depot near the base of Westhaven Nunatak, a rocky peak protruding out of the surrounding ice, its vast bulk hidden beneath thousands of metres of ice. Taking less than two hours to climb the peak, the men were nevertheless exhausted by the end of the day. At an altitude of over 2500 metres, the five hours they spent on its summit while surveying peaks all around were miserable. Ayres, a mountain guide rather than a surveyor, was not altogether impressed with the whole affair and ruefully reflected how they were 'damn cold 8,300ft up a keen wind and we were not moving, carrying a great clumsy tripod up is no joke either'.[14]

From their depot at Westhaven Nunatak, the men travelled north surveying the mountains as far as the Mulock Glacier. They were making wonderful progress and the weather was being generally kind to them. By 14 December, however, during a day with unusually low visibility, they unwittingly entered an area that Ayres felt very uneasy about. The camp was icy and exposed and Ayres, perhaps with a sense of foreboding, went to sleep that night wondering whether it would be wiser to turn back and retrace their route. Waking the next day to much improved weather, the men cast their doubts aside and decided that they could continue pushing their way north.

Ayres and his dog team took the lead. Alert to any signs of crevassing, all of a sudden he knew something had gone horribly wrong. In an instant, he threw himself sideways. Looking up a moment

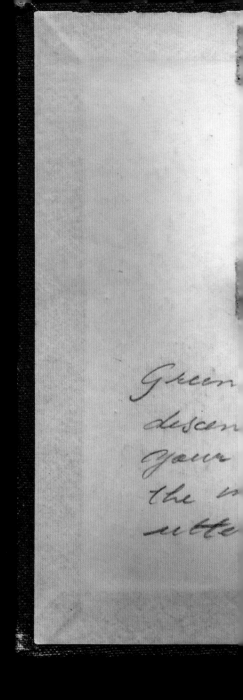

The inside cover of the notebook gifted to Harry Ayres shows an ode to Patsy the dog: 'A prolific breeder, the morals of a harlot, and an utterly charming disposition.'

"PATSY."

d bitch, many of whose

nts will be members of

am. — A prolific breeder,

als of a harlot, and an

charming disposition.

Dear Harry!

In wishing you, Ed. [?] the other kiwis the very best of [?] that the following little draw[?] of some assistance to you in [?] role as "dog-ologist" of the N.[?]

If treated right, a h[?] 'till he drops, — if not — he [?] inefficient means of transport [?] Each dog has his, or her [?] — which pays you to study. [?] during the early stages, you [?] shed tears of exasperation a[?] fury, — but you _MUST_ re[?] golden rule, — _PATIENCE_, and [?] At times you will hate [?] mostly you will love them. [?] good luck, Harry, you'll [?] sin[?]

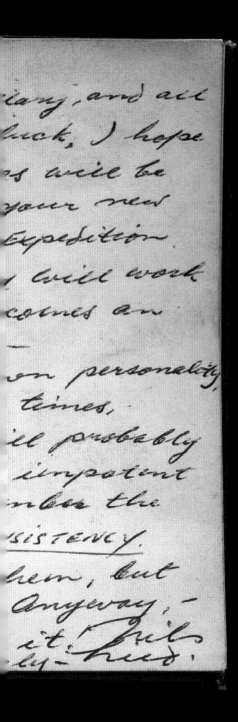

later, he saw that his sledge and all of his dogs had disappeared. He waved frantically to Carlyon, still some distance behind, to warn him of the danger.

A chasm had appeared in the ice and into it had fallen all of Ayres' precious dogs and the sledge. The sledge was stuck in a perpendicular position, about three metres below the surface, its front facing down. The dogs were somewhere under that, and although the men could not see them, occasional whimpers gave hope that some had survived.

Working rapidly, the men secured the sledge to the surface so that it would not fall any further, and then Ayres was lowered down on a rope. Dangling below the front of the sledge were the dogs, still caught in their harnesses. His relief at seeing them was short-lived when he realised that at least one harness was empty. Ayres set to work and he and Carlyon hauled up two of the dogs. After taking a brief rest at the surface, Ayres went down again and they hauled up four more. There were nine dogs in total, and to find the final three it was necessary to descend to the bottom. Carlyon was lowered 21 metres into the pit and, remarkably, found two dogs alive at the bottom. The third one was dead. Skinny, who had been gifted to the expedition by Waimate High School and had narrowly escaped being swept into the Southern Ocean on the voyage south,[15] had slipped from his harness and been killed by the fall.

It was not easy for Carlyon to rescue the final two dogs. Ayres, at the surface, hauled them up by rope, but an overhanging ledge halfway down the crevasse kept snagging them. Carlyon was forced to climb his way up to the ledge to free each dog as it became caught. The accident happened at 1.30 pm, and it was not until midnight that the men could finally sleep. Up early the next morning, they set to work retrieving all the gear from the sledge and, lastly, the sledge itself. For Ayres, however, there was one last trip into the crevasse. At the very bottom, near where Skinny lay, was his wife's Christmas cake. It was a precious treat that she had baked for him in March and had sent to Scott Base, where it arrived in one of the last mail deliveries before the winter.

Ayres was upset about the loss of 'poor Skinny',[16] one of his best dogs, and keenly felt his absence the next day when, after repairing the sledge and dog harnesses, they were able to set off again.

By the end of it all, they had added 25,000 square kilometres of new territory to the maps and had pioneered another route between the Ross Ice Shelf and the Polar Plateau.

The final two weeks before Christmas were spent continuing their surveying of the area north towards the Mulock Glacier and then working their way south again towards the depot at Westhaven Nunatak. Christmas Day 1957 was celebrated with a frozen chicken that Ayres had carried all the way from Scott Base, which they boiled and then roasted. It was delicious. Dessert was, of course, the rescued Christmas cake.

Once back at Westhaven Nunatak, the men set a course south and surveyed as far as the head of the Byrd Glacier. By mid-January it was time to begin the descent of the forbidding Darwin Glacier. In readiness for this, the Beaver arrived on the Plateau on 14 January and disgorged two passengers: Bill Cranfield and Selwyn Bucknell. The pilot and the cook were to have their chance to experience an overland trip in the Antarctic.

Cranfield teamed up with Carlyon, and Bucknell with Ayres, and they set about negotiating their way down to the Ross Ice Shelf. News had come through that the USS *Greenville Victory*, on which many of the men from Scott Base would leave, was due to depart on 25 January. The men had eleven days to get back to Scott Base if they hoped to catch a ride. Descending the glacier was predictably difficult.

Fierce katabatic winds had scoured large sections of the ice, leaving vast swathes of it with unstable snow bridges, sharp ice ridges and surfaces that the dogs' paws could only slide and skitter over. Unable to move camp due to the wind one day, the men were anxious not to be caught on the glacier for too many days. As they descended further, and came to within a few kilometres of the Ross Ice Shelf, the warmer temperatures caused thaw streams to appear and suddenly the men found themselves with wet boots and having to avoid waist-deep water.

On 21 January 1957 the men stepped on to the Ross Ice Shelf and made their way to the Darwin Depot, which had been established by the airmen some weeks earlier. They, and their remaining dogs, were airlifted back to Scott Base the following day.

It was an extraordinary survey trip. For over six weeks, Ayres and Carlyon sledged, climbed, surveyed and geologised. By the end of it all, they had added 25,000 square kilometres of new territory to the maps and had pioneered another route between the Ross Ice Shelf and the Polar Plateau. The expedition had not been without misadventure or sadness but, ultimately, it was a remarkable achievement by two brave and tenacious men.

H. Ayres.

<u>N.Z.A.E.</u> 1956-58

12 Heathes Place Shirley
Ch. Ch.

Bernie Gunn, Richard Brooke, Guyon Warren and
Murray Douglas, just before leaving Scott Base on
the Northern Party journey.

NORTHERN
PARTY

SEVEN

The start was not auspicious. Just a day into the journey one dog had lost the use of an eye, and the men were still smarting from Ed's stern directive exhorting them to work well together.[1]

For Richard Brooke, Bernie Gunn, Guyon Warren and Murray Douglas the release from the confines of Scott Base, and the long winter, must have been liberating both physically and emotionally. It had been a difficult few weeks for some, with lingering uncertainty over the expedition's precise ambit, personal tensions between the men, and the pressure of meticulously preparing equipment and supplies for several months of sledging. Despite all this, however, Warren reflected on the eve of their departure that the Scott Base crew had been 'most of the time a very happy group'.[2]

On 4 October 1957 the men and their dogs set off on a four-month expedition with the aim of surveying as large an area as possible north of Plateau Depot. This would include surveying along the western coast of McMurdo Sound, penetrating inland and upwards to the Polar Plateau and, on the way back down to sea level, completing the survey of the Skelton Glacier area They were a formidable team: Brooke, an Englishman chosen by Fuchs for the New Zealand party, was a surveyor with extensive Arctic polar experience; Douglas was a mountain guide and dog handler; Warren and Gunn were geologists, the latter also a highly skilled mountaineer.

The first three days across well-frozen sea ice to Gneiss Point should have been relatively straightforward and, except for the dogs, it was. Perhaps also suffering from the dark, cold months of relative inactivity, some were grumpy and aggressive. A huge fight broke out among Brooke's dogs. Joe, one of the leading pair and a good hard worker (see photo on page 124), ended up at the bottom of the melee, suffering a nasty bite to one of his eyes. With the eye bloody and swollen, the men were worried about him and treated the wound as well as they could. Fortunately it did heal over time, but Joe never regained sight in that eye.

Reaching Gneiss Point, where a depot had earlier been established,[3] the men wanted to head inland but first they had to find a route up from the sea ice and on to the glacier. It was, in Warren's words, 'quite a picnic'.[4] The slope was steep, icy, and very difficult for the dogs hauling the sledges. The men had to dig channels and steps in the ice so that they could brace the sledges and prevent them slipping down sideways. One at a time, the sledges were forced up the slope, the dogs straining at their traces. Suddenly Brooke let out a roar. Four of his dogs had disappeared down a crevasse. Hauling up the traces, they found only two dogs, Bowers and Fido, were still attached. The other two, whimpering quietly, were crouched in soft snow on a snow bridge 10 metres below the surface.

The men quickly pulled out their ropes and Brooke was lowered into the crevasse. It was extremely narrow, with sheer sides. Joe and Dismal were very excited to see Brooke, energetically struggling through the soft snow to welcome him. Brooke, worried that their movements would cause the snow bridge to collapse, plummeting them further into the crevasse, threaded his arm through their harnesses and, with some difficulty, managed to attach ropes so that they could be hauled back to the surface.

Once order was imposed again, and the men were ready to go, the dogs absolutely refused to move. They could see the gaping crevasse in front of them, and although it was so narrow that they could easily leap it, there was no way they were going near it. Amid much stern encouragement from the drivers to 'get on with it', the dogs broke away and dashed across another part of the crevasse that remained hidden by a snow bridge. Poor Dismal fell in again, but this time his harness stayed attached and they could haul him out.

Seizing the opportunity, Terror, a heavyset dog, managed to free himself from the traces and trotted about, the men fearing for him every time he eluded them and ran across a snow bridge. Eventually he was captured and, with relief, they were all able to move out of the tricky area.

The men kept moving inland until they reached the area near Mount Newell. Although it was 24 kilometres from the sea ice, and over 600 metres high, they were surprised to find a seal carcass. Believing that this was an extraordinary find, and surmising that the biologists at Scott Base would be fascinated, they took it back with them when they returned to the Ross Sea after a few days surveying in the area. It was perhaps this seal or, if not, one very like it, which was to cause much unforeseen difficulty for pilot Bill Cranfield.[5]

Once back at the coast again the men headed north, opting to travel on the sea ice as the only other option was the Wilson Piedmont Glacier which was impassably rough. The sea ice was tricky in its own way. Often sticky, it made very hard work for the dogs pulling the heavy sledges. One of the dogs, Nova, 'much the woolliest dog of the whole … and a very hard worker',[6] simply collapsed and had to be placed on top of the sledge and carried.

Besides being sticky, the sea ice was also prone to cracking. The dogs did their best but sometimes inadvertently led their masters into difficulty. Warren, skiing along beside one of the sledges, was caught off guard when the dogs swung around parallel to a crack between two ice slabs. The sledge's runner sank into the crack, catching Warren's ski and capsizing the entire half-tonne load. Warren's leg was caught underneath, his foot in the crack. Douglas immediately strained to lift the sledge but it was simply too heavy. He screamed out to the others, who were some distance ahead, and Brooke ran back to help. With two men lifting they were able to free Warren who, apart from some bruising, was thankfully not seriously hurt.

It was now mid-October and the men had travelled north as far as Cape Roberts. While they were carrying out surveying work, they were excited to find a cairn built by one of Captain Scott's men in 1911. Digging around in the ice a little, they also uncovered a blubber stove, several items

Another sketch from the notebook on training dogs that was gifted to Harry Ayres.

'...had quite the worst day's sledging yet...Dogs too bad to be true for the first hour or more—could have willingly strangled them one by one.'

GUYON WARREN

of clothing belonging to the old explorers and a couple of bags.

The group kept pushing further north until they reached Granite Harbour. Here they decided to split into two groups temporarily, Warren and Brooke, and Douglas and Gunn, and the men went their separate ways in order to survey a much greater area.

Two weeks later, by now the end of October, 'women trouble'[7] had arrived and was causing mayhem among Warren's and Brooke's dogs. If the men had been entertained by tales of this sort from Miller and Carlyon after their sledging journey the preceding autumn,[8] they were about to find out first-hand that it was no laughing matter. While Allison was very heavily in pup, and kept escaping her traces at night, ZsaZsa was having an upsetting effect on the male members of the pack.

One particularly bad evening barely any sleep was had, even with ZsaZsa tied up well away from any of the others. All night long the dogs kept up a racket, and the following day an exasperated Warren had had enough:

> had quite the worst day's sledging yet. Utterly foul surface—broken and like drying glue, awful to ski on and worse running...Dogs too bad to be true for the first hour or more— could have willingly strangled them one by one. Got even Richard [Brooke] close to complete exasperation, which is something.[9]

The two teams of men and their dogs, their separate surveying trips completed, reunited at Cape Roberts

on 1 November. With the dogs all back together again, peace did not reign. ZsaZsa was tied to the back of the sledge but there was ensuing chaos at every halt. The noise and difficulty was affecting Douglas who, in frustration, vented that the 'dogs went a bit haywire and I got terribly mad'.[10] Four days later the dogs still had not improved and sleep was difficult although, as Warren drily noted, it was not just the dogs who were at fault: 'A lot of row during the night, a fair proportion of it Murray [Douglas], yelling from the other tent, but slept pretty well.'[11]

Douglas was also feeling pressure on a personal level as he struggled to fit in with the other three men. This had been signalled over three months earlier when, within the confines of wintering at Scott Base, he had felt like there was a 'cold war' between Brooke, Gunn and himself.[12] Now, among the complexities and hardships of sledging and camping in Antarctica, and exhausted from lack of sleep and sheer hard physical work, his temper was short. Unfortunately, Douglas felt that there was 'not much love lost between other 3 and I',[13] confirming Ed's suspicion about personality clashes during the expedition and his exhortation to the men to work well together.

Despite the pressures, the men had a job to do and they pushed on. Leaving the sea ice and splitting up into two pairs once more, they headed inland, with Douglas and Gunn working their way up to the head of the Debenham Glacier and

In this sketch from Harry Ayres' notebook, one of the dogs is making away with a whip that his handler has left unattended.

Mummified seal in the Dry Valleys.

Warren and Brooke investigating further to the south. To the men's relief, ZsaZsa eventually returned to her 'usual uninteresting self'[14] and peace reigned for a while.

By 20 November it was time to make a concerted effort to push up to the Polar Plateau. With the four men together again, they headed up the MacKay Glacier. Poor Allison was ready to whelp by this stage, and the men expected to see puppies appear at any moment. Due to her condition the men tended to leave her be if she escaped from her traces at day's end since, rather than wandering off, she would curl herself up somewhere close by and fall asleep.

Returning from surveying up a peak one day, Warren was horrified to see a gash in the side of his tent. He rushed over with horrid visions of a bedful of pups inhabiting his sleeping bag, but fortunately simply found the culprit, Allison, half asleep among the chaos that she had caused. Despite her condition, the men unceremoniously ejected her and, after spending some time mending his tent, Warren went outside and discovered that she had pupped. Wryly noting that 'it was a near miss for my bag',[15] he observed that the pups were stillborn, which was a relief as it would have been necessary to dispose of them anyway.

It was not an easy route up to the Plateau and it took a lot out of the dogs. The men were upset to see how rapidly the dogs lost condition once they were away from the sea ice and its endless supply of fresh seal meat. Once up on the Plateau, and able to receive fresh supplies by plane, they arranged for different dog food to be flown in, and after that the dogs' condition improved markedly.

On the Plateau, the teams headed north and east, sledging and surveying on alternate days. The geologists of the team, Warren and Gunn, were very excited to find coal and fossils during this time. With such a vast area to cover, they did not pause for Christmas Day, climbing a high peak, surveying and only later enjoying an enormous Christmas cake, with candles in the shape of penguins that Douglas had brought with him.

They spent the first two weeks of the New Year surveying and inspecting the southern end of Skelton Neve. Hearing on the radio that the USS *Greenville Victory*, currently in McMurdo Sound, was due to leave for New Zealand in the next few days, the men came to a decision. The work of the Northern Party was all but complete so, with mixed feelings, Douglas and Warren elected to fly back to Scott Base and Claydon flew in to collect them the next day.

Brooke and Gunn, finished with their survey work, turned their attention to a beautiful peak called Mount Huggins. Over 3700 metres high, and part of the stunning Royal Society Range, it was first discovered by Captain Scott's Discovery Expedition of 1901–04 and had never been climbed. Brooke and Gunn were both highly experienced mountaineers and they successfully climbed it on 26 January achieving, in the process, what Hillary later described as quite 'possibly the best piece of mountaineering yet recorded in the Antarctic'.[16]

This mission complete, Brooke and Gunn descended the Skelton Glacier to the Ross Ice Shelf and were flown from Skelton Depot to Scott Base on 6 February. They had spent 127 days out in the field and, together with Warren and Douglas, had sledged over 1600 kilometres and climbed 31 mountain peaks. Altogether, the astoundingly dedicated work of these four men, and their erratic but faithful dogs, had resulted in approximately 50,000 square kilometres of surveyed and geologised territory, between the Mulock and Mawson glaciers, being added to the understanding of Antarctica. A fantastic effort!

After four months away, it must have been a huge shock to the men to return to Scott Base. It was not the same place that they had left. Warren, with an almost tangible sense of sadness, could see that everything was utterly different. As he wrote in his diary:

> Marched into the mess hut which was crammed, and not one single face I'd ever seen before, so just walked quietly out again until we found Murray Ellis to bridge the gap back to civilisation.[17]

The friends and colleagues who they knew so well, and with whom they had shared work, laughter, frustrations, trials and journeys over the past twelve months, were absent. In their place were strangers who now had their own opportunity to carry on the work of the pioneering New Zealand party.

'Marched into the mess hut which was crammed, and not one single face I'd ever seen before, so just walked quietly out again until we found Murray Ellis to bridge the gap back to civilisation.'

GUYON WARREN

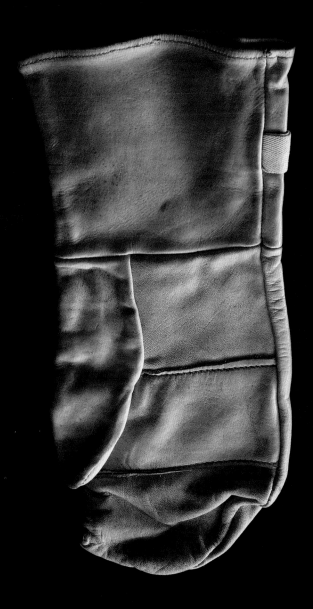
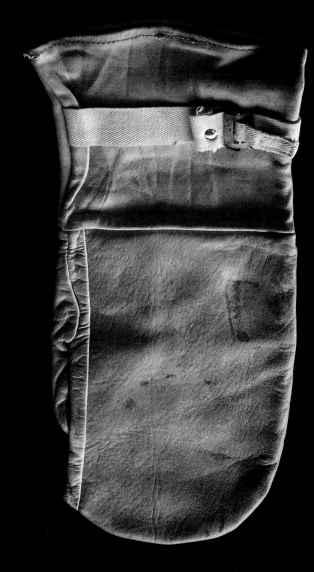

John Claydon came to collect Murray Douglas and Guyon Warren from the Polar Plateau once the work of the Northern Party was all but complete. These are the leather mittens that John wore during the Trans-Antarctic Expedition; they are now part of Canterbury Museum's collection.

JOHN CLAYDON'S MITTENS

The Canterbury Museum collection also includes
this hand-knitted cream jersey, which was worn by
a member of the Trans-Antarctic Expedition. The wool
was originally used for Antarctic sea boot stockings.

KNITTED JERSEY

Sir Edmund Hillary (left) and Dr Vivian Fuchs.

FOLLOWING PAGES: The interior of the box that
held Vivian Fuchs' anemometer (an instrument for
measuring wind speed).

FUCHS:

THE CROSSING FINALE

EIGHT

'HILLARY AND FUCHS: LONDON REPORT OF "RACE TO POLE"'

'FUCHS ON WAY TO POLE: PARTY GOING "FULL BORE"'[1]

E. Fuchs

> ...Fuchs not only refused to break his crossing journey, but advised Hillary that he would no longer need Hillary's assistance and local knowledge...

While the international media played up the notion of a 'race for the Pole' between Fuchs and Hillary, the pair's relationship had not been assisted by communications between Fuchs' and Hillary's parties on the Plateau, which had been irregular and frustrating.

A day before his arrival at the South Pole, Hillary proposed to Fuchs, in light of the slow progress Fuchs was making, that he consider asking Dufek to fly him out from the Pole and return the next season to complete the crossing. Unfortunately this message was inadvertently released to the press and a media storm ensued. Fuchs not only refused to break his crossing journey, but advised Hillary that he would no longer need Hillary's assistance and local knowledge in accompanying him onward from D700 to Scott Base.

Courtesy of the Americans, Hillary and the other tractor men, with the exception of Mulgrew who stayed on at South Pole Station to improve communications with Fuchs' crossing party, flew back to Scott Base. The men were understandably tired and Ed acknowledged that he needed a rest: 'personally I feel the need for a break from the Plateau after nearly four months of tractor travel and there's a lot to do'.[2]

On 18 January 1958, after remaining at Scott Base for a couple of weeks, Hillary accompanied Dufek and a media contingent of nine to fly to South Pole Station in readiness to greet Fuchs' party. They flew over the party and saw outside the tents the lone figure of Ed's old climbing mate, George Lowe, waving to the plane. Two days later, Fuchs and the crossing party arrived at the South Pole. It was a momentous point in the

SNO-CAT

The bright-orange Sno-Cat used by Vivian Fuchs for
the crossing of Antarctica. See also pages 100–101.

journey and they were warmly welcomed by
everyone.

Back at Scott Base from his summer
explorations, however, Warren noted that the
dark cloud of media sensationalism was still
overshadowing the celebrations:

> Bunny at the Pole today. The one dampening
> of the day was to read the sickening stuff that
> has been going out by the ream from the
> Publicity people, trying to make a sensation
> of the strife between Bunny and Ed over the
> question of continuing from the Pole. Ed
> seems to have been tactless at the best, but
> this poisonous muck is horrid to read.[3]

After making arrangements to rejoin Fuchs at
D700 and guide him back to Scott Base, Hillary
returned to Ross Island the following day with
Dufek. Back at the base, Warren, not having seen
Hillary for months, was somewhat shocked by his
condition:

> Ed back from the Pole, and he looks quite
> ghastly. Dreadfully thin though he has put
> on a stone in a fortnight or something. Seems
> quite lifeless and obviously unhappy about the
> whole business. Bunny now says he will travel
> faster and be out early in March, though Ed
> is somewhat unconvinced he can speed up
> so much.[4]

With new vigour, however, and a reduction in the seismic testing that they had been regularly doing en route, the crossing party made much more rapid progress. The journey was not without its dramas, though, and a medical emergency led to a gallant piece of flying from the Americans to drop oxygen bottles to help a team member who was suffering from carbon monoxide poisoning.

On 9 February, Hillary and Claydon flew over five hours in the Beaver to D700 to rendezvous with Fuchs. Hillary was to join the crossing party. His role was to use his knowledge of the route to help guide them safely back to Scott Base. Initially, Fuchs gave up his seat in the cab of the lead vehicle for Hillary, and in due course they found and followed the Ferguson tracks which, despite the effects of Plateau weather, remained prominent after nearly two months. With the two men sharing a tent and working together, with Fuchs driving and Hillary providing direction where he could, the days passed. They celebrated Fuchs' fiftieth birthday with a bottle of whisky Hillary had brought out for the occasion.

Despite the Sno-Cat's impressive power and size, the fact that there were only two seats in the cab meant that extra passengers were subjected to long, boring stints in the back compartment. It was neither insulated nor heated, nor did it have any windows, so that there was only dim light and it was extremely cold even in a sleeping bag. Hillary mused on the ease with which it could have been improved, the consequent improvement in morale, and the different approaches of the British and the New Zealanders to polar travel. He noted:

> However, there was no doubt about it, the traditional British polar traveller felt there was something slightly indecent about being warm and comfortable when a great venture was under way. We spent plenty of time being cold and miserable in the Fergusons, yet I had ensured that whenever we had a break from driving we could retire to a snug warm corner in the caboose and rest in comfort.[5]

Half a century on, Ed still did not recall with fondness those days on the return from D700:

> I was put in the completely blacked-out back compartment and it was only when we got lost, which we did on the odd occasion, that Bunny would call to me, 'Open the door, would you, and find out where we are.'
>
> Of course, I was happy to do this and I didn't have too much trouble finding the route.
>
> Then came the moment I resented slightly, I have to admit, and that was when we started off again and Bunny gestured at the back of the snowmobile and said, 'OK, get aboard and let's head off.'
>
> So I got into the darkness and lay there for hour after hour while Bunny drove—until they got lost again. Then I'd get out, duly find where we were without too much difficulty.
>
> Those many hours, lying in the back of the snowmobile, weren't some of the happiest days on the expedition.[6]

Arriving safely back at Scott Base on 2 March 1958, the crossing party had taken 99 days to traverse the continent—remarkably, one less than Fuchs had estimated. The recorded distance in the official account was 2158 miles (3473 kilometres).[7]

Sir Edmund Hillary is welcomed by a group of Americans on completion of the crossing.

As the remnants of the New Zealand party, together with the crossing party, packed up and headed north on *Endeavour* a new group of men had inhabited Scott Base. Their aim was to continue the scientific work for the remainder of the International Geophysical Year and beyond.

Ken Blaiklock's sledge-meter, which had crossed the continent and read 2043 miles, was packed and went north, but through his generosity was later returned to Scott Base, where it remains.

Flying Officer Bill Cranfield carries a small parcel
of supplies to the Beaver. Mount Erebus can be seen
in the background.

BILL'S
FLYING
ADVENTURES

NINE

William Cranfield—known to one and all as Bill—was the last surviving New Zealand-resident member of the Trans-Antarctic Expedition's New Zealand party to winter over at Scott Base in 1957. Survived only by two members of the IGY party, and one TAE New Zealand party member resident in Britain, Bill died two days before the sixtieth anniversary of the establishment of Scott Base.

At the tender age of 23, Bill was selected to be part of RNZAF Antarctic Flight as the junior flying officer to John Claydon, the squadron leader and chief pilot for the New Zealand party of the TAE. During the New Zealand party's tenure in Antarctica, Bill flew a remarkable 273 hours in route finding and depot laying for Fuchs' TAE

crossing party, Hillary's tractor party and field survey parties. Out of these many aerial episodes, two flights above all others stood out for him. Both were in the small Auster aircraft. The first involved a fight for his life with an unlikely passenger, and the second marked an inauspicious first encounter with a pristine glacier.

The unlikely passenger was a mummified seal. Bill was flying it back from the Dry Valleys to Scott Base for scientific study. Believed to be a couple of thousand years old, the seal was a statuesque 6 feet long, of solid build and as flexible as a plank of wood. The Auster was a dual-control plane, meaning that both the passenger seat and the pilot's seat had control panels in front of them. Prior to taking off, Bill ensured that his passenger

John Claydon and Bill Cranfield at the South Pole.

...he gave graciously of his time and anecdotes, particularly when he divulged, after sixty years, that he was in fact one of the first three New Zealanders to reach the South Pole...

was well strapped in but, somewhere high above McMurdo Sound, the seal slipped forward and jammed its flippers under the passenger control panel in front of it. Suddenly Bill was unable to control the plane. He desperately tried to move the seal but it was stuck fast. Struggling to keep the plane level, Bill (like the seal) was petrified: 'I spent about 40 minutes trying to get control of the plane without success. I was terrified about how I was going to land, but somehow, at high speed, I managed it. It nearly killed me.'[1]

In retrospect, Bill must have realised how close he came to having his fate sealed.

Bill's second memorable flying adventure was a landing on the pristine Hobbs Glacier. With seating for only two people, and carrying radio equipment, batteries, survival gear and tent, there was little room for anything else in the Auster. The plane had no heater but Bill carried a rubber hot-water bottle with him as a container if nature called. In Bill's words:

Fifty-nine years ago last week, on 5th September Ed and I took off in the Auster to examine the sea ice and terrain in the Ferrar Glacier, Butter Point and Marble Point areas. We both wore full outdoor down clothing, gloves, head dress and mukluks and resembled two over-stuffed red mummies. Ed and I are not small people and once strapped in the aircraft could barely move, even with the side door windows bulging part open. As you always got cold feet flying in the Auster, an automatic physiological need for a pee soon arises and gets progressively more urgent with time. To postpone this problem one always cleared one's bladder before strapping into the aircraft. If you were a practising contortionist and could navigate through your clothing you could pee into a rubber hot-water bottle.

On that particular flight Ed's discomfort increased until his eyeballs were bulging. Opposite the mouth of the Ferrar Glacier on our flight back to Scott Base it was obvious that an accident was imminent. Fortuitously we were flying over a piedmont glacier partly fed by the small Hobbs Glacier perched between abrupt mountain walls, which in turn drained from the front of Mt Lister.

Ed was in dire need and eventually asked Bill to land (although it was a risk to the plane) so that he could attend to nature. Bill continued:

There were no obvious crevasses and the surface looked good, so after radioing my intent and a gasp of surprise from the other end and a rather strained acknowledgement, we landed here so Ed could relieve his problem. I must confess that I was nearly as much relieved as Ed for this stop—for it was fast becoming a mutual problem! A pee-stop was a great Kiwi way to celebrate man's first steps on the Hobbs Glacier.[2]

As Bill recalled with a grin when recounting the story, 'My Air Force boss was "not amused".'

Just a few months before his death Bill helped raise the profile of the Antarctic Heritage Trust's campaign to save the original hut that he had wintered in at Scott Base. The media loved the story and he gave graciously of his time and anecdotes, particularly when he divulged, after sixty years, that he was in fact one of the first three New Zealanders to reach the South Pole, ahead of the tractor party. He, with two others, had flown to South Pole Station courtesy of the Americans before Hillary's tractor team arrived.

As a guest of honour at a special dinner, Bill received a standing ovation. The fundraising campaign was called Expedition South.[3] As part of the campaign, the Antarctic Heritage Trust was delighted to arrange a flight for Bill in a vintage Beaver aircraft painted in the same TAE livery he had flown in sixty years ago in Antarctica. Aptly enough, the young pilot, John Evans, had been part of the Antarctic Heritage Trust's conservation scholarship programme with Antarctica New Zealand and the Sir Peter Blake Trust. John had worked one season in Antarctica with the Antarctic Heritage Trust to help conserve the historic huts. He recalled: 'It was really surreal for both of us. Bill hadn't been in this type of plane since the TAE days (60 years ago) but flew it for most of the flight, taking us on a tour of Banks Peninsula. He handled the machine like he had only stepped out of it yesterday, teaching me the odd thing too.'[4]

One of the three Ferguson TE-20 tractors that was
driven to the South Pole, pictured in its display area at
Canterbury Museum.

TRACTOR
JOURNEY
2.0

TEN

The steps of Parliament in Wellington, New Zealand witnessed a reunion over fifty years in the making. Two elderly men looked at each other, paused, and after some time there was a hearty handshake and smiles. It was 2015. The two men were among the few remaining survivors of the New Zealand party that had established Scott Base. For some of them it was the first time they had met again.

During the official event that followed in the Beehive, among the survivors, families, descendants and stakeholders, the New Zealand prime minister launched the conservation plan conceived by the Antarctic Heritage Trust to safeguard the first building at Scott Base. The New Zealand government had asked the Trust to take on responsibility for the site given its proven expertise

in caring for the sites associated with the Antarctic explorers of the 'heroic era'—Scott, Shackleton and Carsten Borchgrevink. With that honour came the dubious responsibility of raising the substantial funds needed to care for the site. On behalf of the Trust, I [Nigel] took to the task with gusto.

To raise awareness and funds to conserve 'Hillary's hut', the Antarctic Heritage Trust conceived and launched Expedition South. It was a quintessential Kiwi journey that honoured the original Hillary-led expedition from Scott Base to the South Pole on plucky Ferguson tractors. On 23 August 2016, two vintage TE-20 Ferguson tractors set off on another tractor journey, along with a modern Massey Ferguson tractor, from the Hillary Trail at Piha, New Zealand. In the lead tractor across

In touring New Zealand the tractors would travel the same distance as Ed's original Antarctic party had covered on their epic tractor journey from Scott Base to the South Pole.

the start line was Ed's son Peter. The tractors' destination was Aoraki Mount Cook village in the South Island, some 2000 kilometres away.

In touring New Zealand the tractors would travel the same distance as Ed's original Antarctic party had covered on their epic tractor journey from Scott Base to the South Pole. The vintage Fergusons were painted red like the original Antarctic tractors, and even featured green canvas cabs. The expedition was led by the Antarctic Heritage Trust's dedicated employee Al Fastier, who would have been a great asset to the TAE if he had been born a generation earlier.

En route the team visited many communities and sites associated with Ed's life, took part in thirty events and visited ten schools. Fifty schools also followed the journey online. Among the highlights were visits to Ed's old primary school in Tuakau, his secondary school at Auckland Grammar, and Sir Edmund Hillary Collegiate in South Auckland where his family home now stands. Here, students simulated pulling one of the tractors across a 'crevasse'.

There were some rough weather days, even appropriately some snow, during the journey, and the occasional mechanical breakdown. Throughout the country the hospitality was outstanding. In Wellington Randal Heke, the original Scott Base foreman who was one of the first New Zealanders, along with Bob Miller and John Hoffman, to sleep at Pram Point in a tent, posed with one of the tractors. A Cabinet minister climbed on the tractor for a photo opportunity. When the expedition

passed through the small rural town of Fairlie there was a procession of twenty vintage and modern Ferguson tractors in a line of honour.

Expedition South arrived safely at Mount Cook on 19 September 2016, nearly a month after leaving Piha. It was 60 years since the TAE trained there before heading to Antarctica. On a flawless spring day the team were greeted at the local airport by TAE family descendants, the media and excited members of the public. Waiting there too were Beaver and Auster aircraft, the former with the TAE livery and the latter with RNZAF, and even a pack of huskies, which had special dispensation to be in the national park. The team of huskies led the tractors, one driven by Peter Hillary, down to the Hermitage hotel over the finish line in the shadow of the statue of Ed.

The expedition raised over $100,000 towards the million dollars overall that the Antarctic Heritage Trust received during the campaign. With the face of Ed on the New Zealand $5 note, along the way people responded enthusiastically to requests to give a 'fiver for the driver'.

The echo of Ed, who himself toured the country to raise support and funds for the TAE, was heard. Fundraising, corporate donations, a grant from the New Zealand Lottery Grants Board and a contribution from the New Zealand government, announced by the then Minister for Culture and Heritage while on site at the hut, ensured a successful conclusion to the appeal in time for the sixtieth anniversary of the construction of Scott Base in January 2017.

Members of the Antarctic Heritage Trust 'Expedition South' team. From left to right: Peter Scott, Lydia McLean, Peter Hillary, Al Fastier and Brian Blyth.

BELOW: The tractor procession en route through New Zealand.

Memorabilia in the living room
at the modern Scott Base.

CONSERVATION

EFFORTS

ELEVEN

In an Antarctic storm, shelter from the wind is your first priority. Given the loss of visibility in blowing snow, colour and contrast can be helpful. In 1957, the intense orange and yellow of Scott Base was a beacon to those caught out by the weather as well as a vibrant counterpoint to the white ice and snow and the black scoria on Ross Island.

Honouring that original intent, and retaining the spirit of place, were paramount to the Antarctic Heritage Trust when it undertook major conservation work on the iconic remnant of New Zealand's first Antarctic presence. Apart from two small buildings that are still used for scientific work—magnetic Hut G (the 'variometer hut') and magnetic Hut H (the 'absolute

hut')—Hut A is all that remains of the original Scott Base built in 1957.

Hut A has had various other names—Mess hut, A hut, TAE hut, TAE/IGY hut and Hillary's hut—but whatever name people associate with it, this small, rectangular, flat-roofed building is an iconic part of Antarctic, and New Zealand, exploratory and scientific history. Forever linked with Sir Edmund Hillary, it is the only remaining building from Fuchs' epic Trans-Antarctic crossing. It was the first building New Zealand constructed in the Antarctic, and the foundation of New Zealand's Scott Base and continuous Antarctic presence for over sixty years.

After its occupation during the first season in 1957 the hut served as Scott Base's kitchen and

The Shacklock 501 range before and
after conservation efforts.

Marcus King's 'High Country Muster'
oil painting after restoration.

mess for a remarkable quarter of a century. In 1982 the mess room was converted to accommodation quarters. In 1989 the major task of relocating the hut was undertaken to enable modern buildings to be erected at Scott Base. At the same time, some conservation work was carried out on the building fabric, internal partitions were reconstructed, and heating was installed. The hut's function changed, and it became a haven in case of fire and a quiet retreat for base staff.

In 2001 the building was listed as Historic Monument No. 75 under the Antarctic Treaty. Sadly, after a period of minimal maintenance significant faults were identified, including leaks in the roof, snow ingress into the outer porch, meltwater pooling under the hut, diesel in the flooring and, most worryingly, the presence of asbestos flaking from the interior walls. Artefacts within the building were showing signs of damage and corrosion. One of two paintings by Marcus

King, which had been gifted by the New Zealand Government Tourist Office at the request of the building's architect, was suffering considerable water damage. Snow had somehow entered the fabric of the building, melted, presumably within the ceiling cavity, and run down the wall.

In 2012 a Memorandum of Understanding regarding the future management of the hut was signed by Antarctica New Zealand, the government agency that manages Scott Base, and the Antarctic Heritage Trust. Upon assuming management of the legacy, the Antarctic Heritage Trust was able to undertake extensive planning and research in preparation for major conservation works.

Following the creation of a detailed conservation plan and with meticulous planning, the Antarctic Heritage Trust's specialist team of twelve worked more than 5700 hours during the Antarctic summer of 2016–17 to restore Hillary's hut in time for the base's sixtieth anniversary celebrations in

January 2017. The following summer the Trust reinstated the original flat-roof design.

Under the leadership of the Trust's programme manager, Al Fastier, the team embraced the challenges. The flaking interior paint was exposing asbestos fibres and the decision was made to remove the asbestos lining from inside the hut. This was the most difficult aspect of the job and a major task, which had to be undertaken by specialists with extensive personal protective equipment. At one point the stripped-out building was no more than an empty shell, and there were doubts as to whether the building would retain its bach-like Kiwi charm when the interior work was completed. Thankfully it did.

The major building conservation work included:

- removing the asbestos wall and ceiling linings;
- painting the interior and exterior of the building;
- reconfiguring the cold porch—the team removed the 1980s cold porch from the hut, retaining the original covered walkway for reuse, with a new cold porch and junction box constructed to the original specifications;
- upgrading foundation timbers and hold-down cables—some 30 anchors to support the hut's rigging were installed;
- removing and reconstructing the partitions to the radio room and Hillary's office;
- repairing roof leaks and installing a new roof over the top of the original roof;
- repairing and reinstating nine chimney flues;
- upgrading the building's electrical services and fire alarm system.

Care was taken to retain and reinstate original building materials—trims, for example—after the asbestos was removed. Where new material was essential, such as new wall linings to replace the asbestos board, modern material was chosen that was as close as possible to the original finish and appearance.

1950S PAINT PALETTE

The original exterior colour scheme was bright—the large wall panels were a vivid yellow; the battens and trim were a vibrant orange. The bright colours enabled pilots to spot Scott Base easily when they flew in. In addition to the exterior, the original architectural plans called for the five main spaces inside the hut—mess room, radio room, Ed's room, the kitchen and cold porch—to be painted in a multitude of colours.

The original paint specified for the interior and exterior was from the company Berger. After much work in the archives and in association with Dulux, which now owns Berger, the original colours were identified and where possible the historic colours and formulas were matched to modern swatches. In some instances the original Bergermaster colour formulas or colours no longer existed. In these cases, with great care flakes of original paint from the building were removed and returned to New Zealand. They were then analysed so the original paint colours could be accurately recreated.

A total of six new custom colours were created by Dulux (see opposite). The Antarctic Heritage Trust had the honour of naming them:

- The exterior yellow was named 'Pram Point' after the geographic location of Scott Base.
- The exterior orange trim, 'Sno-Cat', was named after the bright-orange tracked vehicle Fuchs used for the crossing of Antarctica.

Others included:

- 'Ponder' (exterior flues, yellow)—after the architect of Scott Base, Frank Ponder.
- 'Transmission' (radio room, green-blue)— after the function of the radio room.
- 'Heke' (kitchen cabinetry, mint green)—after Scott Base construction foreman Randal Heke.
- 'Armitage Loop' (Hillary's room, yellow)— after the sea-ice road between Scott Base and the ship.

Painting the exterior in sub-zero conditions was a challenge, with wind chill or storm conditions often making outside work impossible. With persistence and cold fingers, the Antarctic Heritage Trust's team achieved a remarkable transformation, even using brushes rather than rollers to achieve a finish as close as possible to the original. The interior was repainted to the original specifications.

In 2017 the project's colour scheme won the International category of the thirty-first annual Dulux Colour Awards. Today, among the green-painted buildings of Scott Base, the retro colours of Hillary's hut immediately draw attention to it as a unique and very special part of the base.

PRAM POINT

SMOOTH

PONDER

TRANSMISSION

HEKE

ARMITAGE LOOP

Film cannisters on a shelf in Hut A.

PREVIOUS PAGE: The custom colours created
by Dulux for the restoration of Hut A (Hillary's hut)
by Antarctic Heritage Trust.

ARTEFACT CONSERVATION

During the conservation work all the portable objects within the building were removed by the team of artefact conservators before the asbestos removal work commenced. Approximately 550 objects were documented, and conserved as necessary. These included radios, food, clothing and documents from the earliest days of New Zealand's presence in Antarctica. An online record of some of the most iconic artefacts was created by the Antarctic Heritage Trust.

The building's objects include two mid-century Marcus King paintings; one of the New Zealand bush and the other of the high country. The water damage to the oil paintings required specialist conservation. The paintings were packaged and flown from Antarctica to New Zealand in the depths of winter for conservation at the Auckland Art Gallery before being returned to site. It was fitting that the gallery undertook this task for the Trust—in a great piece of symmetry, the principal conservator overseeing the conservation was Ed's daughter, Sarah Hillary.

Some of the heavy and large artefacts needed to be conserved in situ within the building. The two cast-iron stoves required washing to remove dirt, mechanically removing the corrosion and then stabilising the objects through the application of tannic acid and a final coating of microcrystalline wax.

The hut now stands, resplendent in its original colours, in stark contrast to the modern Scott Base. Weathertight, it defies the elements and remains the only building remnant from the TAE. In time, 'Hillary's hut' will take its place beside the revered huts of Scott and Shackleton as a reminder of the intangible spirit that led those men in their quests to explore and discover Antarctica's secrets.

PAGES 179–180: The door from the mess room through to the cold porch.

PAGE 181: Mechanics on the Waterbury heater.

PAGES 182–183: Inside the mess room.

PAGES 184–185: View into the kitchen from the mess room, and vice versa.

ABOVE TO PAGE 189: The kitchen and some of its features.

FOLLOWING PAGE: The No. 2 President cooker, with the snow-melter unit partially visible on the right.

The hut
now stands,
resplendent
in its original
colours, in stark
contrast to
the modern
Scott Base.

FACING PAGE: Instruments in the radio room.

PAGES 192–195: Inside the radio room.

PAGE 194: Dr Vivian Fuchs' anemometer, manufactured
by Kelvin & Hughes Ltd, Basingstoke, United Kingdom.

Honouring the original intent, and retaining the spirit of place, were paramount to the Antarctic Heritage Trust when it undertook major conservation work.

FACING PAGE TO PAGE 205: Inside Ed Hillary's room.

PAGES 206–207: The mess room, with Marcus King's 'Camping Scene' oil painting on the wall to the right.

**ANTARCTIC HERITAGE TRUST
CONSERVATION TEAM, SUMMER 2016–2017**

From left to right: Susan Bassett, Martin Wenzel, Ciarán Lavelle, Geoff Cooper and Lizzie Meek.

Al Fastier (Event Leader), Doug Henderson, Annika Andresen (Antarctic Youth Ambassador), Tony Thrupp and

Gus Anning (New Zealand Antarctic Society volunteers) were absent when the photo was taken.

CONCLUSION

The establishment of Scott Base was quite an achievement. It drew on the skills and experience of countless men, many of whom are consigned to footnotes in history. The New Zealand party of the Trans-Antarctic Expedition and the International Geophysical Year did a remarkable job with limited equipment but armed with the Kiwi practical spirit and number-8 wire mentality.

Ed's audacious bid for the Pole caused consternation, strained friendships and won admirers. It drew headlines, and is now part of the iconic history of Antarctic exploration.

In all the publicity, however, the achievements of the sledging parties were not given the full credit and recognition they deserved. Some of the epic journeys by Miller and Marsh, Ayres and Carlyon, Douglas and Warren, Gunn and Brooke were worthy of the heroic age of exploration. From establishing new routes from the Ross Ice Shelf on to the Polar Plateau, to the mapping of over 100,000 square kilometres of new terrain, and first ascents of dozens of peaks, theirs were exceptional achievements. The longest sledge journey ever undertaken in history, up to that time, was made by Miller and Marsh.

The efforts of Claydon and Cranfield flying small aircraft in challenging terrain were essential to the success of the expedition and the crossing party. The IGY scientists' 'indigenous' research, which Trevor Hatherton yearned for, and the establishment of monitoring programmes and experiments that still run today, creating some of the longest unbroken records in the Antarctic, are invaluable.

It was a boys' own adventure, and it truly was boys only in the 1950s. The wildly differing agendas of science and exploration led to tensions, even without Ed's own agenda of reaching the South Pole. Inevitably there were pressures on relationships and friendships. Personalities, as they always do, played a part. The confines of an Antarctic winter strained relationships. Meticulous planning, and a dose of good luck here and there, all added to the mix. For all this the leader, Sir Edmund Hillary, deserves both credit for the successes and accountability for the failings.

Notwithstanding the pressures, the accomplishment that tops all else is the fact that so much was achieved by a team of dedicated men who saw opportunity and embraced it, each in his own way.

In the final wash-up, however, history shows that these men laid the foundation for the continuous occupation of Scott Base in Antarctica. They paved the way for generations of men and women to live in, experience and enjoy the wonders of Antarctica in the pursuit and support of science and conservation. This is their lasting legacy.

As the New Zealanders' first Antarctic winter settled in, Trevor Hatherton, head of the IGY science party, mused in his diary: 'Ed says what a pity the Americans don't devote say 5% of their effort to "exploration". What is this "exploration" that people talk about? Is it anything concrete?'[1]

Exploration is both concrete and meaningful. Exploration is more than a mindset; it is a core human instinct manifesting in curiosity and inquiry.

Over half a century on, in answering the question, exploration is both concrete and meaningful. Exploration is more than a mindset; it is a core human instinct manifesting in curiosity and inquiry. It is the powerful drive to better understand the world around us and to discover, challenge and experience new things. The timeless spirit of exploration enticed people of the Pacific, and centuries later from Europe and beyond, to traverse the world's greatest ocean and settle in New Zealand. And it is the same spirit that opened Antarctica to the world. Over 650 people from numerous countries were eager to experience it when, in 1956, they applied for positions in the New Zealand party.

Even if it was not at the forefront of their minds, Hillary, Hatherton and all the members of the TAE and IGY had this spirit in spades. In a complex, overcrowded and changing world, the same spirit of exploration might be a necessary trait as we look to the next generation to unlock the secrets of our world and ensure the survival of our species.

ABOVE AND FOLLOWING PAGE:
The door to Magnetic Hut G.

PAGE 213: An historic fluxgate
magnetometer (which measures
change in magnetic field) showing
N–S and E–W axis in Magnetic Hut G.

PAGES 214–215: A non-magnetic theodolite
(surveying instrument) with a fluxgate
sensor mounted on it in Magnetic Hut H.

THIS PAGE: A Stevenson meteorological screen housing a weather station—the longest-running continuous scientific record at Scott Base.

FACING PAGE: The exterior of a modern container in the Scott Base environs.

Magnetic Hut G (far left) and Magnetic Hut H (centre, in the background) are still in use today by scientists. Together with Hut A (Hillary's hut) they are the only buildings remaining from the original Scott Base.

TIMELINE[1]

	4 OCT	20 OCT	31 OCT	24 NOV	25 NOV	15 DEC
FUCHS' CROSSING PARTY				Depart Shackleton Base		
HILLARY'S TRACTOR PARTY	Depart Scott Base	Arrive Skelton Depot	Arrive Plateau Depot		Establish Depot 480	Establish Depot 700

The Scott Base site is prepared in early 1957.

1958

22 DEC	4 JAN	20 JAN	7 FEB	17 FEB	23 FEB	27 FEB	2 MAR
Arrive South Ice Base		Arrive South Pole	Arrive Depot 700	Arrive Depot 480	Arrive Plateau Depot	Arrive Skelton Depot	Arrive Scott Base
	Arrive South Pole						

BIOGRAPHIES

This section lists members of the New Zealand party of the Trans-Antarctic Expedition and International Geophysical Year, as well as significant others.[1]

FIELD PARTY

Hillary, Sir Edmund P. (1919–2008) KBE, Polar Medal, Hubbard Medal National Geographic Society, Commander Merite Sportif, Star of Nepal 1st Class, US Cullum Geographical Gold Medal, Royal Geographic Society's Founder Medal, Explorers Club Medal. Leader Ross Sea Party TAE and IGY. Educated Auckland Grammar School, Auckland University College. Hon. LLD University of Victoria British Columbia 1969, Victoria University of Wellington 1970. Nine honorary doctorates. Apiarist. Served in WWII in the Pacific, as navigator on Catalina flying boats. Gained mountaineering experience in the Southern Alps. Joined the first all-New Zealand Garhwal Himalayan Expedition 1951; the British Everest Reconnaissance 1951; the British Cho Oyo Expedition 1952; was the first person to reach the summit of Everest, with Tenzing Norgay, on the British Everest Expedition 1953, for which he was knighted; led the NZ Himalayan Expedition 1954. These experiences secured his leadership of the NZ Antarctic Expedition 1956–58. The success of that expedition was followed by numerous expeditions in the 1960s and '70s, including a Ganges jetboat expedition from the Bay of Bengal across India and into the Himalayas.

He made significant contributions as a philanthropist and humanitarian, building his first school in the Mount Everest area in 1961, and in 1964 he set up the Himalayan Trust to improve services and infrastructure in Nepal by developing clinics, hospitals, airfields and schools there. The Sherpas called Hillary 'Burra Sahib', meaning 'big boss' or 'big sir'. He served as the New Zealand High Commissioner to India, Nepal and Bangladesh from 1984 to 1989. He was the Honorary President of the American Himalayan Foundation, an Honorary Member of the New Zealand Alpine Club, the Explorers Club New York and Hon. President 1985–87, and President of Volunteer Service Abroad. He returned to Antarctica in 1967 and led a team whose members climbed Mount Herschel. In 1985 he joined astronaut Neil Armstrong on a flight to the North Pole, making him the first person to have reached both poles and the summit of Everest. Hillary appears on New Zealand's $5 note.[2]

Miller, J. Homes (Bob, later Sir) (1919–1986) OBE. Surveyor and Deputy Leader Ross Sea Party TAE. Waimate High School (Dux); Victoria University Wellington BA, PhD. Polar Medal. NZ Institute of Surveyors' Fulton Medallion. Mrs Patrick Ness Award of the Royal Geographical Society. Entered Public Service in 1936, joined the Department of Lands and Survey in 1938, surveying unmapped areas of Fiordland. Served in Middle East during WWII with 12th Field Regiment of Artillery; injured in action and invalided home to New Zealand. Consulting Registered Surveyor since 1948. In 1949 he led the mapping survey party of the New Zealand-American Fiordland Expedition; in 1950 he completed a survey of the Bounty and Antipodes islands. During the TAE, he surveyed vast areas of the Trans-Antarctic Mountains by dog sledge with George Marsh, with one journey of 1680 miles (2740 km) being the longest dog sledge journey on record in Antarctica. Executive Officer, Antarctic Division of the DSIR (1958–59). Resumed survey practice in Wellington in 1959. Led the 1963–64 Northern Victoria Land expedition, the last major Antarctic expedition where dogs were used. Member of the Ross Dependency Research Committee from its inception in 1958, chairman 1971–83; president of the New Zealand Antarctic Society (1960–63); Member of the New Zealand Geographic Board (1968–86), and chaired the Royal Society of New Zealand's National Committee for Antarctic Research (1970–76). Also involved with the Outward Bound Trust, and the World Wildlife Fund. Chairman of the Nature Conservation Council, and of the Australian and New Zealand Schools Exploring Society, and served on the world executive (1969–74) of the Commonwealth Association of Surveying and Land Economy (CASLE). Fellow of the NZ Institute of Surveyors and Royal Institute of Chartered Surveyors. In 1979 he was knighted for his services to the Ross Dependency, conservation and surveying and was awarded an honorary doctorate in science from Victoria University.[3]

Ayres, Harry H. (1912–1987) OBE. Polar Medal. Mountaineer, dog handler. Born in Christchurch. At 16 he moved to the West Coast and worked on a farm, then with a Buller Gorge railway construction gang; and on the new road linking Fox to Franz Josef glaciers. While gold prospecting and doing farm work at Waheka, Fox Glacier, he gained climbing experience and became a glacier guide. At Mount Cook he undertook a three-year training programme and qualified as Chief Guide, and was Chief Guide at the Grahams at Franz Josef. Served with the New Zealand Third Division in the Pacific during WWII. Resumed guiding at the Hermitage in 1946, climbing all the major peaks of the Southern Alps, Mount Cook eight times and Mount Tasman five times, earning a reputation as New Zealand's greatest climber. After TAE, he was appointed Chief Ranger for Mount Cook National Park;

was then manager of the Automobile Association's camping ground at Hanmer, and later head gardener at Mona Vale, in Christchurch.[4]

Brooke, Lieutenant Commander Richard (b. 1927) Surveyor. Polar Medal. Educated at Royal Naval College, Dartmouth. Naval surveyor who saw service in WWII off the Normandy beaches in HMS *Warspite*. In 1948–50 was Third Officer on RRS *John Biscoe* (later HMNZS *Endeavour*) on supply voyages to Falkland Islands Dependencies scientific bases. From 1950–51 he served aboard the HMS *Scott*, a hydrographic survey vessel. From 1952 to 1954 he was with the British North Greenland Expedition. Brooke was one of the two Englishmen selected by Dr Fuchs for the New Zealand Party of TAE.

Carlyon, Roy A. (1932–1980) Assistant Surveyor-Navigator. Polar Medal. Born in Wellington, he spent his early years in the Cook Islands, at Pahiatua and Auckland. Educated at Wanganui Technical College (1949–50) and received a Bachelor of Engineering (Civil) in 1954 from Canterbury University College. He worked for the Ministry of Works, surveying traverses for new bridges between Pukaki and the Hermitage. When selected for TAE was on the staff of New Zealand Railways in the district engineer's office at Wanganui. Outdoor interests included deer stalking and climbing in Mount Cook region.

Douglas, Murray (1927–1992) Mountaineer. Polar Medal. Born and educated in Dunedin. A keen member of the Otago Tramping Club. When he was selected for TAE, he was working at the Hermitage at Mount Cook as assistant chief guide. His key role in the expedition was as mountaineer, but he also served as assistant dog handler, tractor driver and mechanic. He was originally selected as a member of the summer party, but Hillary kept him south as the twenty-third member of the wintering party. After the expedition, he worked on the Ohau skifield for the Mount Cook and Southern Lakes Tourist Company. In the 1960s he moved to Otematata where he bought the information centre, also racing a launch called *Miss Benmore*. In the early 1980s he worked as caretaker of the camping ground at Gore Bay near Cheviot.[5]

Ellis, Murray R. (1924–2005) Engineer. Polar Medal. Explorers Club Medal (New York). Attended Waitaki Boys' High School and Canterbury University where he graduated with a Bachelor of Engineering (Mechanical). Joined the Royal New Zealand Navy Volunteer Reserve in 1942 as an elite Fleet Air Arm pilot, completing his training in New Zealand, England and the USA. After the war he earned a degree in engineering and joined the family firm, Dunedin-based bedding company Arthur Ellis Ltd, becoming manager and later managing director, a position he held until 1980. He was involved in many community organisations: he was vice-president of the New Zealand Alpine Club; president of the Otago-Southland Manufacturers Association; Dunedin coordinator for the Duke of Edinburgh Award Scheme; director of the Dunedin Rotary Club; president of the Dunedin West Probus Club and a senior member of the Brevet Club. He was also a foundation member of the Himalayan Trust and helped build schools, provide water supplies and build access tracks in the Everest district of Nepal.[6]

Gunn, Bernard (Bernie) M. (1926–2008) Geologist. McKay Hammer Award of the Geological Society of New Zealand, Polar Medal, Royal Geographical Society Bronze Medal. Worked in Otago as a high-country shepherd where he developed a keen interest in mountaineering, before going to Otago University in 1951 to study for a Bachelor of Science in geology. He became a skilled mountaineer and gained experience as a guide at Franz Josef and went on to make a record of nearly 100 ascents in the Southern Alps. He was also an experienced photographer and map maker with the use of aerial photographs. He collaborated with the RNZAF and government departments to make the first complete photographic survey of the Southern Alps from the air. Also a competent radio operator and motor mechanic. After the expedition he received a PhD from Otago University and went on to teach at Tulane University in Louisiana and the University of Montreal. His research focused on petrological topics and also retrieval and plotting of geochemical data, computer simulation of magnetic processes and computer data storage. He returned to New Zealand in the late 1970s and taught briefly at Seddon

High School, then worked as a consultant and computer salesman, eventually becoming managing director of Kaipara Hills Forest.[7]

Marsh, Dr George W. (1925–1988) Polar Medal (TAE clasp). Medical officer and experienced dog handler. Born in Dorrington in the UK. Qualified in 1950 at St Bartholomew's Hospital, London as physician and surgeon. Employed by the Falkland Islands Dependencies Survey between 1951 and 1954. During this period he served on RRS *John Biscoe* (later HMNZS *Endeavour*). In addition to his duties as medical officer, he was in charge of the base's fifty dogs. Along with Miller, Marsh made the longest dog-sledge journey on record in Antarctica during the expedition—of 1680 miles (2740 km) during which the two men mapped previously unknown parts of the Trans-Antarctic Mountains and Polar Plateau. He was a haematologist and went on to become a consultant at Hertford Hospital in England. He was a regular attendee of Antarctic Society events.[8]

BASE PARTY

Balham, Dr Ronald (Ron) W. (1921–1999) Polar Medal. Medallion of the Royal Geographical Society (London), honorary member of the Explorers Club (New York). Biologist and meteorologist. Educated at Wellington College; awarded a Master's Degree at Victoria University of Wellington and a PhD from University of Missouri. He joined the Meterological Office in 1939–42. Served with the RNZAF in 1943–44, then in the overseas service coast-watching on the sub-Antarctic Auckland and Campbell islands; this involved observational work on auroral and ionospheric activity. He joined the Research Section of the Wildlife Branch of the Department of Internal Affairs in 1947. In the 1950s he returned to academic study, eventually setting up the country's first course in animal ecology. He published on a wide variety of topics, including waterfowl, Antarctic meteorology and fossilised seals.[9]

Bates, James (Jim) G. (1924–2011) Polar Medal. Diesel mechanic. Bates was a skilled engineer and partner in a Morrinsville mechanical engineering business, with extensive knowledge of petrol and diesel engines. He was also an inventor—his designs included a honey-filling machine, honey extractor, high-pressure rotary valve pump, a new type of pipe-drain digger, and he built his own astronomical telescope. He served in the 16th Reinforcements of the New Zealand Expeditionary Force in Egypt, Italy and Japan during WWII. He had extensive alpine experience including 30 ascents of Mount Ruapehu (mostly on skis), and of building huts in alpine conditions. After TAE, he ran a company supplying shipbuilding components, inventing and developing new boat designs.[10]

Bucknell, Ernest (Buck) Selwyn (1926–2001) Polar Medal. Cook. Educated at Hutt Valley Memorial Technical College, Petone. Served an apprenticeship and qualified as a metal fitter and turner and toolmaker in New Zealand Railways. He joined the Wildlife Division of the Department of Internal Affairs in 1950 as a deer culler. In the three years before TAE he worked on possum research in charge of the Wildlife Division's Orongorongo research station. Bucknell originally tried for the expedition as a diesel/electrical mechanic, but eventually was enlisted as the cook. He brushed up his skills during a crash course at the New Zealand Army's cooking school at Waiouru, and became experienced at parcelling supplies for airdropping. After the expedition he returned to wildlife work, becoming involved in the Canada goose control programme. In 1984 he was appointed manager and keeper of the Maud Island wildlife reserve for seven years until his retirement in 1991.[11]

Warren, Guyon (1933–2003) Geologist. Polar Medal. Educated at Christ's College, Christchurch and Canterbury University College, graduating with honours in geology in 1955. He had experience in geological mapping for the New Zealand Geological Survey. One of the youngest in the group, he was also a capable surveyor, cook and photographer.

RADIO OPERATORS

Gawn, John Edward (Ted) (1917–1988) Radio Operator. Polar Medal. Educated at Christian Brothers' School, Dunedin, Marist Brothers' Tasman Street School, Wellington and Wellington Technical College. A Merchant Navy officer with considerable experience as a radio operator and expert at Morse code. Served in WWII aboard the hospital ship *Maunganui* on voyages to the Middle East and in the Pacific. From 1947 to 1952 he served as radio technician with the New Zealand Broadcasting Service at Titahi Bay, Wellington, and Opapa, Hawke's Bay. When selected for the expedition, he was serving on the inter-island steamer *Hinemoa*. He returned to Antarctica in the early 1960s, and went on to work for the Post Office, then the Union Steam Ship Company. After his retirement, he devoted time to teaching his skills to radio amateurs.[12]

Mulgrew, Peter David (1927–1979) CPO RNZN. British Empire Medal, Polar Medal, JP, FRGS, AMIRE. Chief radio operator. Educated at Hutt Valley Memorial Technical College, Royal Naval College, Greenwich, and Harvard Business School. He joined the Navy in 1945 and qualified in all aspects of naval radar and radio communications. He completed a course in London with the Royal Geographical Society in surveying, mapping, field astronomy and instrument adjustment, and was elected a Fellow of the Society in 1947. He returned to New Zealand in 1947 and served as a Petty Officer Radio Mechanic and by 1954 was appointed Chief Radio Electrician. He was selected for TAE as an experienced operator of ionospheric equipment. His association with Hillary continued and in 1960 he was radio-operator and climber in a Himalayan Scientific and Mountaineering Expedition with Hillary, but suffered pulmonary oedema and lost both his lower limbs to frostbite. He retired from the Royal Navy in 1963; participated in a 1964 Himalayan schoolhouse expedition, and in a 1966 Himalayan hospital expedition. He became the New Zealand manager of Pye Telecommunication. In 1966 he became the general manager of L.J. Fisher and Co., and in 1978 the corporate general manager of Alex Harvey Industries Ltd in Auckland. A keen yachtsman, he represented New Zealand in the world One Ton Cup yachting championships in Sydney in 1972, and sailed around Cape Horn the following year. He died in the 1979 Mount Erebus plane crash.[13]

Claydon, John R. (1917–2014) AFC. Polar
Medal. Sqd. Ldr and Chief Pilot. Educated
Christchurch Technical High School; joined
RNZAF as an airman in 1936; received 'special
distinguished pass' with commission as Flying
Officer. Served in WWII in the Pacific with No. 14
Squadron; then as administrator Air Department
Wellington, and Command of Flying Training
School Wigram. Following appointment to TAE
attended No. 6 Squadron Hobsonville for training
on Auster float plane. Visited Weddell Sea as
member of New Zealand Advance Party in the
55/56 season, and during TAE provided support
for Ross Sea Party depot laying. In 1959–60 he
was OC Administration at Ohakea; 1960–63 Air
Attaché at the New Zealand Embassy in
Washington; 1963 Director of Operations RNZAF;
Honorary ADC to Governor-General 1964–65;
1964–65 OC Administration at Wigram; 1967–70
Assistant Airport Manager at Christchurch
International Airport, and 1970–72 Airport
Management Advisor for the Asian Development
Bank in Nepal. Retired to Christchurch.[14]

Cranfield, William Joseph (Bill) (1933–2017)
AFC. Polar Medal. Flying Officer and junior pilot
RNZAF Antarctic Flight 1956–58. Educated at
Waitaki Boys' High School and Christ's College
1948–50. Learned to fly with Air Training Corps
and Canterbury Aero Club; entered RNZAF in
1954. When selected for TAE, was an instructor at
Flying Training Schools at Taieri and Wigram with
over 1000 hours of flight experience. During TAE,
flew 273 hours in route finding and depot laying
for Fuchs' crossing party and in direct support of
Hillary's tractor party and three separate field
survey parties; returned to Antarctica in the
1959–60 season, effecting a difficult rescue after
the crash of the Beaver near the Beardmore
Glacier. Spent 28 years in various command, staff
and flying positions, flying fixed and rotary wing
aircraft, retiring as Wing Commander in 1983.
Started a walnut orchard and pottery business at
Chertsey. Retired to Christchurch.[15]

Tarr, Sergeant Lawrence Walter (Wally)
(1924–2012) Aircraft mechanic. Polar Medal,
British Empire Medal. Educated Hamilton

Technical College and Druleigh College,
Auckland. He was a member of the Air Training
Corps, before entering the RNZAF in 1943,
training as a flight mechanic and engine fitter.
He had wide overseas experience, serving in Fiji
between 1947–49, and in Cyprus with No. 14
(Fighter) Squadron between 1952–54. He was
a sergeant stationed at Ohakea RNZAF Base,
with a reputation for skilled work and high
standards, when he volunteered for TAE and was
selected as an engine fitter. In 1961 he took officer
training and served as an engineering officer at
Hobsonville and Wigram. He also served in
the United States overseeing production of the
RNZAF's fleet of Hercules aircraft. He retired
from the RNZAF in 1976 and built light
commercial aircraft.[16]

Hatherton, Dr Trevor (1924–1992) Polar Medal.
OBE. FRSNZ Hector Memorial and Prize. Leader
of IGY party. Born in Yorkshire, England,
educated at University of Birmingham and Acton
Technical College. Awarded BSc Hons (Special
Physics), University of London, and Diploma
Geophysics from the Imperial College of Science
and Technology in London. Came to New Zealand
as a National Research Scholar 1950 to study with
the geophysics unit of the DSIR, work that led him
to attain a PhD from University of London. He
returned to New Zealand and joined the DSIR as
a geophysicist in 1953, and was chosen to lead
New Zealand's IGY party. Wide recognition as an
authority on Antarctic science led to study as a
Commonwealth Fund Harkness Fellow at the
California Institute of Technology, then as a
Fulbright Fellow at Stanford University. In 1965
he became superintendent of the Geophysical
Survey and, in 1967, Director of the Geophysics
Division at DSIR. Elected a Fellow of the Royal
Society of New Zealand in 1969 and served on
their council as secretary and later president.
Awarded a DSc from the University of London
in 1973. Chairman of the Ross Dependency
Research Committee 1983 to 1988.[17]

Gerard, Vernon B. (b. 1924) Physicist IGY party.
Polar Medal (Royal Presentation by Queen
Mother). Born and educated in Christchurch,

gaining a BSc in 1946, and an MSc Hons in 1947. Employed by the DSIR Magnetic Observatory in Christchurch from 1942; saw short war service in the artillery, 1944–45; was stationed in Apia Observatory in 1949; and was later principal scientist at the Physics and Engineering Laboratory (PEL) where he made the first atomic clock and gas laser to be operated in New Zealand. Extensive experience in magnetic observations; installed, and operated without a break, the Geomagnetic Observatory instruments at Scott Base during the 1957 year; returned to Scott Base in early 1959 to recalibrate them after the 1958 year. On sabbatical leave to work with National Physical Laboratory (NPL), London, 1960–63, and later worked in Geophysics and Geodesy Dept, University of Cambridge in England (1975), returning to work at the DSIR until retirement in 1981. Made a Fellow of the British Interplanetary Society in 1948 and a Fellow of the Institute of Physics in 1963. Author of many published scientific papers in journals in New Zealand and overseas, also the book *With Hillary at Scott Base: A Kiwi Among the Penguins*, 2012.[18]

MacDonald, Peter (b. 1926) Technical Officer, IGY party. Polar Medal. Educated at Wellington Boys' College and Victoria University. Appointed to Geophysics Division of DSIR in 1946; spent eight months in Australia in 1951 working for the Bureau of Mineral Resources. In 1954 trained as a teacher, but rejoined the DSIR on selection for IGY, and spent the rest of his career (until retirement in 1989) in Geophysics Division. Published widely, on IGY investigations (including the movement of the Ross Ice Shelf), and especially on his later work in defining the extent of geothermal fields. This was mainly in New Zealand, but included work in the Philippines in the 1980s under a New Zealand government aid programme; took part in UN Symposia on the Development and Use of Geothermal Resources in the 1970s, and did work for the UN in Chile and El Salvador. His name was given to the Macdonald Bluffs in Antarctica. Lives today in retirement in Wellington.

Orr, Herb (1928–1978) Technical Officer IGY party. Polar Medal. Born in Christchurch, and educated at Wellington Technical College, and Victoria University (BSc). In 1943 he joined the radio development laboratory of the DSIR. In 1946, after a year's service in the RNZAF, he joined the staff of the Dominion Physical Laboratory, transferring in 1948 to the Geophysics Division of the DSIR. Went overseas in 1951 and returned to DSIR where he was engaged in seismic observations. His post-TAE career is not presently known.

Sandford, Neil (1930–2013) Technical Officer IGY party. Polar Medal. Born in Raetihi, and attended Wanganui Technical College 1944–48. Joined Radio Section of Post and Telegraph Department where he installed remote area communications links and radio systems. Held a First Class certificate in radio technology. In 1949 spent six months in Rarotonga working on the reconstruction of the radio station. He was chosen for TAE to undertake the operation, maintenance and observation of the panoramic isosonde and pulse transmitter. After the expedition, he moved to Australia to work at deep space tracking stations in Cooby Creek, Honeysuckle Creek and Tidbinbilla. He was involved in various NASA space programmes including the Apollo moon landings, for which he built the Apollo spacecraft simulator. Retired in 1998, but continued to teach his skills to others at the Oxley Region Amateur Radio Club.[19]

BASE DESIGN AND CONSTRUCTION

Heke, Randal (b. 1928) Foreman, Construction Unit. Polar Medal. Educated at Cambridge District High School. Joined Ministry of Works, serving a carpentry apprenticeship, and working at various hydroelectric projects, successively at Karapiro, Maraetai, Tekapo and Roxburgh; then as a building supervisor in the Pacific in Niue, Western Samoa and Chatham Islands. After TAE, returned to Scott Base in later seasons for other building projects, and later had extensive involvement with New Zealand embassy buildings around the world; he finished his career with the ministry as chief building officer in head office. He is a life member and past president of the Antarctic Society, and lives today in retirement in Waikanae.

Mitchell, Ron (b. 1925–d. unknown) Architectural draughtsman. Educated at Petone Primary School and Petone Technical College. Employed by Architectural Division of Ministry of Works for ten years and responsible for providing advice on technical aspects of the construction of building at Scott Base. Was a keen yachtsman.

Ponder, Frank (1916–2001) QSM. Architect, Ministry of Works. During the Depression obtained employment in an architect's office, followed by the Housing Department, and in late 1940s transferred to the Government Architect's Office in the Public Works Department. Responsible for design of Scott Base. Later undertook extensive architectural work for the Department of Island Territories; consulting architect for the Department of Civil Aviation. In 1962 he was chairman of the International Symposium on Polar Buildings at Colorado University. In 1964 he founded the Urban Development Association Inc.[20]

OTHERS WHO PLAYED MAJOR ROLES

Dufek, George J. Rear Admiral (1903–1977) Commander USN Operation Deep Freeze. Navy Distinguished Service Medal, Legion of Merit with two Gold Stars, World War II Victory Medal, Korean Service Medal, Croix de guerre, Legion d'honneur. Educated at Reserve Officer Training School, Annapolis 1921–25 and Naval Air Training Station Pensacola, Florida, 1932–33. Naval aviator and polar expert. Served in WWII and Korean War; Rear Admiral R.E. Byrd's Third Antarctic Expedition 1939–41; USN Operation Highjump 1946–47; appointed Commander USN Operation Deep Freeze 1954 Task Force 43; established Little America Station at Kainan Bay and the later named McMurdo Station. Landed at South Pole 31 October 1956. Retired 1959. Director of the Mariners' Museum in Newport News, Virginia.

Fuchs, Vivian Ernest (Bunny) (later Sir) (1908–1999) Polar Medal. Royal Geographical Society Founder's Gold Medal. Silver Medal of the Royal Society of Arts. Born Isle of Wight, and educated Brighton College in Sussex and St John's College Cambridge, earning a MA and PhD. Studied natural history with an emphasis on geology. Participated in the Wordie Expedition to Greenland 1929 followed by exploration in Africa. Served in WWII in Africa and Europe. Joined Falkland Islands Dependencies Survey 1947–50 completing three consecutive winters in Antarctica; appointed Director FIDS Scientific Bureau 1950; began planning for a Trans-Antarctic Expedition 1955. Following expedition to Weddell Sea wintered at Shackleton Base 1957 and departed for crossing of Antarctica 24 November 1957; arrived Scott Base 2 March 1958. Fuchs was Director of FIDS, subsequently the British Antarctic Survey, from 1958 to 1973. He was knighted in 1958, served successively as president of the International Glaciological Society, the British Association for the Advancement of Science and the Royal Geographical Society.[21]

Helm, Arthur (1914–1998) MBE, FRGS, FRPSNZ. Liaison and postal officer Scott Base. Educated Riverton Primary School. Joined New Zealand Post Office 1930. Served in WWII for the First Echelon of the 2 NZEF. Returned to the Post Office in 1945 and transferred to Dunedin to attend the University of Otago; graduated BA Dickinson College USA; MA Victoria University. He returned to New Zealand in 1949 and was stationed at Wellington as Post Office archivist and historian. In 1955 he was seconded to the Public Service as secretary to the Ross Sea Committee. He was made a Fellow of the Royal Geographical Society in 1956, and was secretary of the Antarctic Place Names Committee for seven years from 1957. He then transferred to Industries and Commerce Department. In 1959–60 he became private secretary to the Leader of the Opposition, Rt Hon. Keith Holyoake. He was with the Tourist and Publicity Department 1961–69 and with the Cook Islands Tourism Authority 1969–72. From 1973 to 1978 he worked for the National Mutual Life Association. He was the New Zealand director and founder NZ American Field Service Scholarships; president of PEN; and an honorary secretary, then vice president, of the New Zealand Antarctic Society. He published numerous books.[22]

Supplies are unloaded from HMNZS *Endeavour* at
McMurdo Sound in early 1957. The adventure was just
beginning for many of the men described here.

Hoffman, John H. (Jack) (1923–1991)
Explosives expert. Hoffman's knowledge of
explosives combined with his expertise in drilling
led to his selection as a summer party member of
the IGY team for 1956–57. He joined the DSIR
in 1947 and became a Grade 1 Technician with
Geophysics Division. This work involved field
work and drilling for Geophysical Survey and
work at hydroelectric sites and for geothermal
investigations in Central North Island. During
1955–56 he was in charge of field staff establishing
and erecting Geophysics Division's observatory
at Chateau Tongariro.

Kirkwood, Capt. Harry (b. 1925–d. unknown)
OBE. DSc RN. An experienced ice captain,
appointed Commander of HMNZS *Endeavour*.
Born in the UK. Served on royal research ship
Discovery for six years until WWII, visiting the
Ross Sea on several occasions. He twice
circumnavigated the Antarctic. For several years
he commanded the Falkland Islands Dependencies
Survey's ship *John Biscoe*; renamed HMNZS
Endeavour, it became the Antarctic Research
support vessel. Kirkwood landed the New Zealand
section of the expedition, along with the material
needed to construct Scott Base. After the TAE he
continued with a career in the Pacific and Hong
Kong, and received an MBE in 1977.

ACKNOWLEDGEMENTS

FACING PAGE: View from the modern Scott Base to Hut A (Hillary's hut) and south to Mount Discovery.

Thanks to the team at Allen & Unwin who enthusiastically embraced the idea of the book, particularly to Melanie Laville-Moore for her continued support and to Jenny Hellen who skilfully and gently cajoled and supported us through this project. Thanks also to Leanne McGregor, whose dedication got the book to completion, to editor Susan Brierley and proofreaders Mike Wagg and Leonie Freeman, and to Alan Deare and Dave McDonald of Area Design for the stunning design and attention to detail.

A massive thanks to Kerry Watson for extensive research on diaries and the TAE in general. Her careful eye and attention to detail, together with her considerable effort in compiling the storyline, were critical. The book would never have reached fruition without her dedication, support and effort.

Very special thanks go to the descendants and family members of original expedition members who shared so willingly of their memories and memorabilia. Particular thanks to the Hillary family and especially to June Lady Hillary and Peter Hillary who each supported the book project from the outset. Special mention and thanks go to Kate Carnaby (née Hatherton) for access to Trevor Hatherton's diaries and memorabilia, Graeme Ayres for access to Harry Ayres' diaries and memorabilia and sharing of stories, Jan Fullerton (née Miller) for access to a copy of Bob Miller's diaries and for locating and lending such wonderful memorabilia, to David Ellis for permission to photograph Murray Ellis' jacket, and to Helen Cranfield for her support.

Sincere appreciation to Peter Beggs, staff at Antarctica New Zealand and the Scott Base teams for their support of the Trust and of Jane's photographic endeavours in Antarctica, and for access to Antarctica New Zealand's photographic archives. Particular thanks to Bailey Jeffery-Butler for assistance provided to Allen & Unwin with imagery from the archives.

Thanks to Anthony Wright and the team at Canterbury Museum, especially Sarah Murray, Jennifer Storer, Joanna Sczpanski and Lisa McDonald for access to the diaries of Guyon Warren and Murray Douglas and for access and permission to photograph TAE artefacts in the museum collection.

Thanks go to the Commodore Hotel in Christchurch and the wonderful and generous Patterson family for their support in accommodating Jane Ussher when photographing in Christchurch and for their enthusiasm for all things Antarctic.

We acknowledge and thank Antarctic Heritage Trust chair Mark Stewart and fellow trustees. To the wonderful team at Antarctic Heritage Trust, thank you. Specific mention of Karen Clark, Helen Keimig, Lizzie Meek, Al Fastier, Robyn Brunton and Francesca Eathorne for your contributions. The Antarctic Heritage Trust conservation plan authors, led by Chris Cochran, and the conservation teams, led by Al Fastier, who worked on the hut in the 2016–17 and 2017–18 seasons did an amazing job. Thank you all.

Thanks go to the New Zealand Antarctic Society, and to Dr Margaret Bradshaw in particular, for access to its archives in Christchurch.

A big thanks to Natasha Lamont and the team at Dulux whose research and work, together with that of Chris Cochran and the team at Antarctic Heritage Trust, made the colours of the 1950s reappear in the Antarctic.

Finally, I have used my best endeavours to try and accurately represent and fact-check the stories, journeys and images. However, inevitably on a subject so well studied and researched by so many people over so long and, indeed, with some conflicting primary sources, there may well be errors or omissions.

NOTES

PREFACE

1 Sir Edmund Hillary, personal communication with the author, Remuera, Auckland, early 2000s.

TWO
POLITICS, PREPARATIONS & PARTIES

1 Sir Edmund Hillary, *No Latitude for Error*, London: Hodder & Stoughton, 1961, p. 13.
2 Sir Vivian Fuchs and Sir Edmund Hillary, *The Crossing of Antarctica*, London: Cassell, 1958, p. 22.
3 Hillary, *No Latitude for Error*, p. 46.
4 Diary of Trevor Hatherton, 28 December 1955.
5 A.S. Helm & J.H. Miller, *Antarctica*, Wellington: Government Printer, 1964, p. 97.
6 Diary of Trevor Hatherton, undated, 1956.
7 Diary of Harry Ayres, 7 January 1956.
8 Helm & Miller, *Antarctica*, p. 105.
9 Diary of Harry Ayres, 31 January 1956.
10 Ibid., 1 February 1956.
11 Personal communication, G. Ayres (son of H. Ayres), to author, 6 April 2018.

THREE
THE ADVENTURE BEGINS

1 Sir Edmund Hillary, *No Latitude for Error*, London: Hodder & Stoughton, 1961, pp. 50–51.

2 W. Frank Ponder, *A Man from the Ministry: Tales of a New Zealand Architect*, Christchurch: Wenlock House, 1996, p. 97.
3 Ibid., p. 97.
4 Ibid., pp. 97–98.
5 Cable from Hillary to Helm, quoted in A.S. Helm & J.H. Miller, *Antarctica*, Wellington: Government Printer, 1964, p. 131.
6 Hillary, *No Latitude for Error*, p. 62.
7 Diary of Bob Miller, 31 December 1956.
8 Ibid., 1 January 1957.
9 Diary of Harry Ayres, 1 January 1957.
10 Ibid., 5 January 1957.
11 Diary of Guyon Warren, 25 December 1956.
12 Hillary, *No Latitude for Error*, p. 72.
13 Helm & Miller, *Antarctica*, p. 23.
14 Bill Cranfield, personal communications with author, October 2016.
15 Diary of J.H. (Bob) Miller, 8 January 1957.
16 Hillary, *No Latitude for Error*, p. 77.
17 Diary of Guyon Warren, 8 January 1957.
18 Diary of Trevor Hatherton, 19 January 1957.
19 Ibid., 21 January 1957.
20 Diary of J.H. (Bob) Miller, 14 January 1957.
21 Ibid., 20 January 1957.
22 Diary of Guyon Warren, 31 January 1957.

23 Ibid., 21 February 1957.
24 Diary of Trevor Hatherton, 21 February 1957.
25 Ibid.
26 Hillary, *No Latitude for Error*, p. 80.
27 Ibid., p. 82.
28 Ibid., p. 87.
29 Helm & Miller, *Antarctica*, p. 169.
30 Diary of J.H. (Bob) Miller, 8 February 1957.
31 Ibid., 9 February 1957.
32 Ibid., 10 February 1957.
33 Ibid., 28 February 1957.
34 Diary of Harry Ayres, 28 February 1957.

FOUR
LIFE AT SCOTT BASE

1 Diary of Trevor Hatherton, 23 February 1957.
2 Ibid.
3 Ibid., 28 February 1957.
4 Diary of Guyon Warren, 24 and 26 February 1957.
5 Diary of Trevor Hatherton, 28 February 1957.
6 Diary of Guyon Warren, 28 February 1957.
7 Ibid., 26 February 1957.
8 Ibid., 4 March 1957.
9 Sir Edmund Hillary, *No Latitude for Error*, London: Hodder & Stoughton, 1961, p. 100.
10 Diary of Guyon Warren, 7 February 1957.
11 Diary of J.H. (Bob) Miller, 17 March 1957.

12 Diary of Guyon Warren, 17 March 1957.

13 Peter MacDonald, letter to Antarctic Heritage Trust, 2014.

14 A.S. Helm & J.H. Miller, *Antarctica*, Wellington: Government Printer, 1964, pp. 210–11.

15 Diary of Guyon Warren, 26 May 1957.

16 See Chapter Five 'The Tractor Journey'.

17 Diaries of Guyon Warren and Murray Douglas, 24 April 1957.

18 Diary of Guyon Warren, 26 April 1957.

19 Hillary, *No Latitude for Error*, p. 105.

20 Diary of Guyon Warren, 22 February 1957.

21 Diary of Harry Ayres, 16 and 17 June 1957.

22 Personal communication with June (Lady) Hillary, who in 1957 was married to Peter Mulgrew, 28 March 2018.

23 Bill Cranfield, personal communication with author and Chris Cochran, 11 July 2013.

24 Diary of Guyon Warren, 13 April 1957.

25 Ibid., 1 March 1957.

26 Letter from Peter MacDonald to Antarctic Heritage Trust, 12 April 2014.

27 Bill Cranfield, personal communication with author and Chris Cochran, 11 July 2013. Out of curiosity, the Antarctic Heritage Trust recreated the 'moose's milk' recipe and served it at an event in Parliament to launch the Conservation Plan for safeguarding Hut A (Hillary's Hut) at Scott Base. Despite the attendance of remaining New Zealand-resident survivors of the expedition who might have been able to extol the virtues of 'Moose's Milk', it is fair to say that politicians, from the prime minister down, descendants and supporters were not immediate fans. It was obviously a taste acquired in its day from necessity.

28 Diary of Trevor Hatherton, 19 May and 7 June 1957.

29 Diary of Harry Ayres, 2 and 4 June 1957.

30 Ibid., 23 June 1957.

31 Diary of Guyon Warren, 16 October 1957.

32 Hillary, *No Latitude for Error*, p. 140.

33 Diary of Guyon Warren, 29 May 1957.

34 Diary of Harry Ayres, 29 May 1957.

35 Diary of Guyon Warren, 21 June 1957.

36 Diary of Harry Ayres, 21 June 1957.

37 Hillary, *No Latitude for Error*, pp. 106–7.

38 Diary of Guyon Warren, 9 September 1957.

39 Ibid., 29 September 1957.

40 See Chapter Seven 'Northern Party'.

FIVE
THE TRACTOR JOURNEY

1 Sir Edmund Hillary, *No Latitude for Error*, London: Hodder & Stoughton, 1961, p. 191.

2 Diary of Guyon Warren, 6 August 1957: 'Also in process of construction is the "caboose" in which the four or five of the tractor party will live, supposing it doesn't blow over in the first good wind. High powered calculations assuming about 15 unknowns are supposed to prove it will need more than 100 knots to tip it, but it certainly doesn't look like it.'

3 Ibid., 13 March 1957.

4 A.S. Helm & J.H. Miller, *Antarctica*, Wellington: Government Printer, 1964, p. 165.

5 Diary of J.H. (Bob) Miller, 22 October 1957.

6 Hillary, *No Latitude for Error*, p. 127.

7 Ibid., p. 129.

8 Ibid., p. 130.

9 Ibid., p. 138.

10 The Geographic South Pole is commonly known as the South Pole. It differs in location from the South Geomagnetic Pole which, in 1957, was close to the location chosen by the Russians for their base called Vostok Station. The South Geomagnetic Pole is approximately 1300 kilometres from the South Pole.

11 Hillary, *No Latitude for Error*, p. 104.

12 Helm & Miller, *Antarctica*, p. 420.

13 Hillary, *No Latitude for Error*, p. 149.

14 Ibid., p. 161.

15 Ibid., p. 163.

16 Helm & Miller, *Antarctica*, p. 268.

17 Hillary, *No Latitude for Error*, p. 139.

18 Ibid., p. 101.

19 Diary of Guyon Warren, 16 April 1957.

20 Hillary, *No Latitude for Error*, p. 178.

21 Ibid., p. 178.

22 Ibid., p. 188.

23 Ibid., p. 193.

24 Ibid., p. 194.

25 Helm & Miller, *Antarctica*, p. 333.

26 Ed Hillary, speaking to staff and assembled guests, including the author, at Scott Base, January 2007. Recounted in Tom Hunt, 'Edmund Hillary's defiant South Pole dash', 3 January 2015, stuff.co.nz

27 Ibid.

SIX
DOGS ON THE PLATEAU

1 Diary of J.H. (Bob) Miller, 1 November 1957.

2 See Chapter Five 'The Tractor Journey' for a description of Miller and Marsh's climb up the Skelton Glacier.

3 Diary of J.H. (Bob) Miller, 8 November 1957.

4 Diary of Harry Ayres, 8 November 1957.

5 Diary of J.H. (Bob) Miller, 14 November 1957.

6 Diary of Harry Ayres, 14 November 1957.

7 See Chapter Five 'The Tractor Journey'. John Claydon, flying in supplies to stock D480, was given incorrect coordinates (largely due to Ed's trouble with navigation instruments) and was struggling to find the site of the depot. He and his passenger observed the tracks left by the dogs and their sledges and, following those, came upon D480.

8 Diary of J.H. (Bob) Miller, 30 November 1957.

9 Ibid., 4 December 1957.

10 A.S. Helm & J.H. Miller, *Antarctica*, Wellington: Government Printer, 1964, p. 274.

11 Diary of J.H. (Bob) Miller, 15 December 1957.

12 Ibid.

13 Diary of Harry Ayres, 5 December 1957.

14 Ibid., 12 December 1957.

15 See Chapter Three 'The Adventure Begins'.

16 Diary of Harry Ayres, 26 December 1957.

SEVEN
NORTHERN PARTY

1 Diary of Guyon Warren, 3 October 1957: 'Ed had a word with the four of us leaving tomorrow, to "discuss" his little directive … seems to imagine we are going to come to blows each morning deciding whether to survey or geologize.'

2 Ibid., 3 October 1957.

3 Hillary, Bates, Ellis, Mulgrew and Orr had used tractors during a spring journey to leave food and fuel supplies at Butter Point and Gneiss Point, to be used during sledging journeys later in the season.

4 Diary of Guyon Warren, 7 October 1957.

5 See Chapter Nine 'Bill's Flying Adventures'.

6 Diary of Guyon Warren, 13 October 1957.

7 See Bob Miller's diary entry in Chapter Three 'The Adventure Begins'.

8 See Chapter Three 'The Adventure Begins' for Miller and Carlyon's difficulties with an 'on heat' Tukluk during their reconnaissance trip across the Ross Ice Shelf in February 1957.

9 Diary of Guyon Warren, 1 November 1957.

10 Diary of Murray Douglas, 1 November 1957.

11 Diary of Guyon Warren, 4 November 1957.

12 Diary of Murray Douglas, 21 July 1957.

13 Ibid., 3 November 1957.

14 Diary of Guyon Warren, 7 November 1957.

15 Ibid., 22 November 1957.

16 Sir Edmund Hillary, No Latitude for Error, London: Hodder & Stoughton, 1961, p. 228.

17 Diary of Guyon Warren, 20 January 1958.

EIGHT
FUCHS:
THE CROSSING FINALE

1 Headlines from The Press on 27 December 1957 and 28 December 1957 respectively.

2 Sir Edmund Hillary, No Latitude for Error, London: Hodder & Stoughton, 1961, p. 218.

3 Diary of Guyon Warren, 20 January 1958.

4 Ibid., 21 January 1957.

5 Hillary, No Latitude for Error, p. 237.

6 Ed Hillary, speaking to staff and assembled guests, including the author, at Scott Base, January 2007. Recounted in Tom Hunt, 'Edmund Hillary's defiant South Pole dash', 3 January 2015, stuff.co.nz

7 Sir Vivian Fuchs and Sir Edmund Hillary, The Crossing of Antarctica, London: Cassell, 1958, p. 293.

NINE
BILL'S FLYING ADVENTURES

1 Antarctic (The Publication of the New Zealand Antarctic Society), December 1996, p. 146.

2 Transcript of speech by Bill Cranfield during the Antarctic Heritage Trust's fundraising dinner in aid of the conservation of the TAE hut. The Commodore Hotel, Christchurch, New Zealand, 14 September 2016.

3 See Chapter Ten 'Tractor Journey 2.0'.

4 John Evans, personal communication with author, October 2016.

CONCLUSION

1 Diary of Trevor Hatherton, 29 April 1957.

TIMELINE

1 A.S. Helm & J.H. Miller, Antarctica, Wellington: Government Printer, 1964, Appendix V, pp. 422–23.

BIOGRAPHIES

1 Biographies taken from the Antarctic Heritage Trust Conservation Plan, 2015, editor Chris Cochran, which acknowledges the principal source: A.S. Helm & J.H. Miller, Antarctica: The story of the New Zealand Party of the Trans-Antarctic Expedition, Wellington: Government Printer, 1964, pp. 71–92. Additional research and writing was carried out by Miranda Williamson, February 2014. Biographies updated by Karen Clarke, March 2018, and additional research by Nigel Watson, April 2018. Individual sources are noted below.

2 'Hillary, Sir Edmund Percival', in Notable New Zealanders: The Pictorial Who's Who, Auckland: Paul Hamlyn Ltd, 1979, p. 208; 'Hillary, Edmund Percival', Shaun Barnett, Dictionary of New Zealand Biography, Te Ara—the Encyclopedia of New Zealand, updated 30 October 2012, URL: www.teara.govt.nz/en/biographies/6h1/hillary-edmund-percival; Diana Dekker, 'Spirit and Essence of NZ', Dominion Post, 12 January 2008, pp. W2–W3.

3 'Miller, Sir Holmes', in Notable New Zealanders, p. 319; 'Miller, Joseph Holmes', Robin Ormerod, Dictionary of New Zealand Biography, Te Ara—the Encyclopedia of New Zealand, updated 20 November 2013, URL: www.TeAra.govt.nz/en/biographies/5m50/miller-joseph-holmes; 'Sir Joseph Miller', Timaru Herald, 12 December 1986, p. 2.

4 'Ayres, Horace Henry', Graham Langton, Dictionary of New Zealand Biography, Te Ara—the Encyclopedia of New Zealand, updated 4 June 2013, URL: www.teara.govt.nz/en/biographies/5a28/ayres-horace- henry; Trish McCormack, 'Harry Ayres: Epitome of park qualities', The Press, 26 December 1987, p. 18; 'Harry Herbert Ayres OBE', the Canterbury Mountaineer 1987, Journal of the Canterbury Mountaineering Club, no. 53, pp. 65–66; 'Harry Ayres one of NZ's greatest mountaineers', Wanganui Chronicle, 14 August 1987, p. 12.

5 'Obituary: Mr Murray Douglas', Timaru Herald, 12 March 1992, p. 2.

6 'Mr Methodical quietly achieved', Otago Daily Times, 12 February 2005, p. 39; 'Murray Roland Ellis',

New Zealand Alpine Journal, 2005, vol. 57, pp. 158–59.

7 *New Zealand Alpine Journal*, 2008, vol. 60, p. 133; *Geological Society of New Zealand Newsletter*, no. 147, November 2008, pp. 34–35.

8 'Obituary', *Polar Record*, vol. 25, no. 153, April 1989, p. 156; 'Polar trekker dies, 63', *Evening Post*, 1988, p. 16.

9 'Adventurer-academic a pioneer', *Evening Post*, 23 September 1999, p. 7; 'Balham, Ronald Walter', *Notable New Zealanders*, p. 21.

10 Barry Clarke, 'Harsh memories on ice', *Sunday Star-Times*, 23 January 2000, p. A6.

11 'Ernest Selwyn Bucknell', Bill Cranfield, *Antarctic: The Journal of the New Zealand Antarctic Society*, vol. 19, no. 1, 2001, p. 107; 'Mr Jack of all trades', *The Press*, 3 May 2001, p. 7.

12 'NZ South Pole expedition man dies', *Evening Post*, 6 May 1988, p. 18.

13 'Mulgrew, Peter David', Graham Langton, *Dictionary of New Zealand Biography*, Te Ara—the Encyclopedia of New Zealand, updated 3 December 2013, URL: www.teara.govt.nz/en/biographies/5m61/mulgrew- peter-david; 'Mulgrew, Peter David', *Notable New Zealanders*, p. 333; 'Peter Mulgrew', *New Zealand Alpine Journal*, vol. 33, 1980, pp. 122–23.

14 John Henzell, 'Tales of the Antarctic originals', *The Press*, 13 January 2007, p. D5; 'Claydon, John Richard', *Notable New Zealanders*, p. 95.

15 From biographical notes prepared by Daniela Liggett, University of Canterbury, 2012.

16 Obituary: 'Practical perfectionist played role in famous South Pole race', *Waikato Times*, 23 June 2012, p. B4.

17 Karen Brown, 'Directors plan happy return to coal-face', *Evening Post*, 23 April 1984, p. 16; 'Hatherton, Trevor', James W. Brodie, *Dictionary of New Zealand Biography*—Te Ara – the Encyclopedia of New Zealand, updated 8 October 2013, URL: www.teara.govt.nz/en/biographies/5h10/hatherton-trevor; 'Trevor Hatherton', *The Proceedings of the Royal Society of New Zealand*, The Royal Society of New Zealand, Wellington, 1996, pp. 119–23.

18 Alan Samson, 'Antarctic Expedition reunion', *Dominion*, 15 January 2000, p. 3; also information provided by Vern Gerard to Antarctic Heritage Trust, May 2014.

19 'Silent key: Neil Sandford vK2EI', *ARNSW Newsletter*, 17 March 2013, www.arnsw.org.au

20 'Ponder, William Frank', *Notable New Zealanders*, p. 370.

21 'First to cross Antarctica', *Evening Post*, 18 November 1999, p. 5; 'Obituary, Sir Vivian Fuchs', Scott Polar Research Institute, www.spri.cam.ac.uk/people/fuchs/; 'Obituary: Sir Vivian Fuchs', *The Independent*, http://www.independent.co.uk/arts-entertainment/obituary-sir-vivian-fuchs-1125583.html

22 Peter Kitchin, 'Appetite for travel led to 200 countries', *Evening Post*, date unknown, p. 5; Alistair Rowe, 'Carried war dispatches by camel: The hundred interests of Arthur Helm', *Evening Post*, 14 June 1969, p. 35; Ngaire Hopper, 'First to answer the call', *Evening Post*, 30 September 1989, p. 32; 'Helm, Arthur Stanley', *Notable New Zealanders*, pp. 201–2.

ADDITIONAL IMAGE CREDITS

Antarctic Heritage Trust: pages 171 (bottom) and 174 (top and bottom)

Antarctica New Zealand Pictorial Collection: pages 7 (Ed_Hillary), 20 (ANZSC1170.6), 37 (TAE 0572), 56–57 (TAE 1156), 84 (ANZPC0130.18), 103 (TAE 1067), 106 (TAE 1132), 111 (ANZSC0003.1), 114 (bottom left, TAE 1218), 114 (top right, TAE 1066), 124 (TAE 0713), 146 (TAE 1013), 158 (TAE 1117), 162 (ANZPC0149.12), 163 (TAE 1242), 164 (TAE 0402), 166 (ANZSC0339.19), 218–219 (TAE 367) and 229 (TAE 0576)

Antarctica New Zealand Pictorial Collection, photographer John Claydon: pages 12 (TAE 1257), 31 (TAE 1261), 41 (TAE 1246), 42 (TAE 352), 45 (TAE 385), 58 (TAE 1039), 64 (TAE1957Winterover003) and 96 (bottom right, TAE 1037)

Antarctica New Zealand Pictorial Collection, photographer Geoffrey Lee Martin: pages 32 (TAE 1073), 63 (TAE 1217), 87 (TAE 1015), 96 (top left, TAE 787) and 110 (TAE 1001)

Antarctica New Zealand Pictorial Collection, photographer Dr Graeme Midwinter: page 43 (Slide 012)

Canterbury Museum: pages 88 (Stan McKay Collection, 1980.192.116, image reproduced courtesy of the Star Media) and 102 (19XX.2.471)

Stuff / *Timaru Herald*: page 171 (top)

Every effort has been made to trace the copyright holders of historic images and to obtain their permission for the use of copyright material. The publisher apologises for any errors or omissions in the above list and would be grateful if notified of any corrections that should be incorporated in future reprints or editions of this book.

BIBLIOGRAPHY

Ayres, H. Diaries 1956–58

Cochran, C., Fastier, A., Meek, L., Harrowfield, D. and Watson, N. *Conservation Plan: Hillary's Hut, Scott Base*. Christchurch: Antarctic Heritage Trust, 2015

Douglas, M. Diaries 1956–58

Fuchs, Sir V. and Hillary, Sir E. *The Crossing of Antarctica: The Commonwealth Trans-Antarctic Expedition 1955–58*. London: Cassell, 1958

Hatherton, T. Diaries 1956–58

Helm, A.S. and Miller, J.H. *Antarctica: The Story of the New Zealand Party of the Trans-Antarctic Expedition*. Wellington: Government Printer, 1964

Hillary, Sir E. *No Latitude for Error*. London, Hodder & Stoughton, 1961

Lowe, G. and Lewis-Jones, H. *The Crossing of Antarctica: Original Photographs from the Epic Journey that Fulfilled Shackleton's Dream*. London: Thames & Hudson, 2014

Miller, J.H. Diaries 1956–58

Ponder, W.F. *A Man From the Ministry: Tales of a New Zealand Architect*. Christchurch: Wenlock House, 1996

Quartermain, L.B. *South From New Zealand: An Introduction to Antarctica*. Wellington: R.E. Owen, 1964

Thompson, J. *Climbing the Pole: Edmund Hillary & the Trans-Antarctic Expedition 1955–1958*. Norwich: The Erskine Press, 2010

Warren, G. Diaries 1956–58

ABOUT THE AUTHORS

A qualified lawyer, Nigel Watson is the Executive Director of the Antarctic Heritage Trust. The Trust cares, on behalf of the international community, for the first expedition bases left in Antarctica's Ross Sea Region. This includes the iconic bases left by expeditions led by Robert Falcon Scott, Ernest Shackleton and Sir Edmund Hillary.

Nigel conceived and has overseen the Ross Sea Heritage Restoration Project—the world's largest cold-climate heritage conservation project—and has led expeditions to Antarctica for the past eighteen seasons.

With a background in mountaineering and skiing, he has skied across the Greenland icecap, telemarked Shackleton's route across South Georgia Island, skied at the North Pole and climbed extensively, with ascents of Mount Scott in Antarctica as well as Aoraki Mount Cook, Mount Aspiring and numerous other 3000-metre peaks in New Zealand.

Nigel is an authority on Antarctic history and is the co-author of the acclaimed *Still Life: Inside the Historic Huts of Scott and Shackleton* with Jane Ussher and a contributor to Assouline's *South Pole: The British Antarctic Expedition 1910–1913* by Christine Dell'Amore.

Jane Ussher is well known and respected for her documentary work as a photographer, and is regarded as one of New Zealand's foremost portrait photographers. For twenty-nine years she was the chief photographer at the *New Zealand Listener*, after which she took up a freelance career working with various magazines and producing several books.

In January 2009, at the invitation of Antarctica New Zealand and the Antarctic Heritage Trust, Jane travelled to the Antarctic and spent over four weeks on the ice photographing the historic huts of Scott and Shackleton. Those images were published in the book *Still Life* and subsequently became the basis for an immersive Antarctic Heritage Trust exhibition that travelled nationally and internationally.

Jane's other published books include the award-winning *Coast: A New Zealand Journey*, *Face to Face*, *Worship: A History of New Zealand Church Design* and *Islands: A New Zealand Journey*.

In 2009 Jane was made a Member of the New Zealand Order of Merit for services to photography, and was also inducted into the Massey University Hall of Fame.

First published in 2018

Allen & Unwin
Level 3, 228 Queen Street
Auckland 1010, New Zealand
Phone: (64 9) 377 3800
Email: info@allenandunwin.com
Web: www.allenandunwin.co.nz

83 Alexander Street
Crows Nest NSW 2065, Australia
Phone: (61 2) 8425 0100

A catalogue record for this book is
available from the National Library
of New Zealand.

ISBN 978 1 76063 357 8

Design by Area Design
Set in Plantin, ITC Johnston
and Sporting Grotesque
Maps by Area Design
Printed and bound in China by Hang Tai
Printing Company Limited

10 9 8 7 6 5 4 3 2 1